PSYCHOANALYTIC CONCEPTS OF DEPRESSION

Psychoanalytic Concepts Of Depression

By
MYER MENDELSON, M.D.
The University of Pennsylvania
Philadelphia, Pennsylvania

CHARLES C THOMAS • PUBLISHER
Springfield • Illinois • U.S.A.

CHARLES C THOMAS • PUBLISHER

BANNERSTONE HOUSE

301-327 East Lawrence Avenue, Springfield, Illinois, U.S.A.

Published simultaneously in the British Commonwealth of Nations by

BLACKWELL SCIENTIFIC PUBLICATIONS, LTD., OXFORD, ENGLAND

Published simultaneously in Canada by

THE RYERSON PRESS, TORONTO

With THOMAS BOOKS careful attention is given to all details of manu-
facturing and design. It is the Publisher's desire to present books that are
satisfactory as to their physical qualities and artistic possibilities and appropriate for their particular use. THOMAS BOOKS will be true to those laws of
quality that assure a good name and good will.

Printed in the United States of America

TO MY WIFE

PREFACE

Despite several historical reviews of depression there has as yet been no survey of this subject comprehensive enough to place recent developments in theory in their proper perspective. Zilboorg (1941a) devoted comparatively little space to depression in his history. Aubrey Lewis's (1934a) scholarly study of the concept of melancholia up to 1930 did not neglect psychoanalytic contributions but his summary of them was relatively cursory as was his treatment of Adolf Meyer's views and influence. Lewin (1950) included a brief literary and historical survey of depression in his book *The Psychoanalysis of Elation* but his interest was of course primarily in the euphoric and excited pole of the manic-depressive dichotomy. Bellak's (1952) summary of the psychoanalytic contributions to the theory of manic-depressive psychosis was also relatively brief. Perhaps Garma's (1947) was the most detailed psychoanalytic review of a historical type whereas Fenichel's (1945) chapter on the subject in his text-book remains the most comprehensive and authoritative exposition of the Freudian concepts of depression up to the time of his survey. But none of these reviews has attempted to study in any meaningfully critical way the pattern of the historical development that has led to the present still imperfect understanding of this problem.

This is the task that I have set myself in this study. I have not undertaken to propose any new theory of depression. I have instead confined myself to the critical examination of the concept of depression as it has evolved and as it prevails today.

To help the reader follow my treatment of this theme I believe that a brief preliminary sketch would be helpful. Although this book is primarily devoted to a consideration of psychoanalytic concepts of depression there is an introductory chapter relating these psychodynamic theories to the broader field of clinical psychiatry. In this chapter, after reference is made to the pre-Kraepelinian thought on the subject of depression, the Kraepelinian contribution is dealt with together with subsequent European and American developments.

In the next two chapters I have presented the theoretical models of the psychoanalytic workers who have contributed most to the theory on depression. These writers are Abraham, Freud, Rado, Gero, Melanie Klein, Bibring, Edith Jacobson, Mabel Blake Cohen and her colleagues as well as authors whose contributions have been of lesser importance. I have presented the views of these writers in roughly chronological order and have tried to show how at every point their theories were rooted in what had been developed previously and at the same time were subtly shaped by contemporary psychoanalytic theory.

In the next chapter attention is focused on specific themes in the development of this body of theory. The perspective here is cross-sectional rather than longitudinal as in the preceding two chapters. The themes considered are constitutional and psychological factors predisposing to depression, the question of whether there is a central anxiety situation in human development and its relation to depression and the role that obsessional elements, aggression, orality and introjective mechanisms play in depression.

This chapter is followed by one on diagnostic considerations in which relatively neglected aspects of this subject are considered. In this chapter an attempt is made to emphasize the variety of depressive reactions, and to stress the implications of this in any theory of depression.

The next chapter is one in which the psychoanalytic literature on treatment of depression is carefully and critically reviewed.

A concluding chapter then follows in which I reflect on the scientific workmanship of this body of psychoanalytic literature both from the point of view of its accomplishments and of its failings. I finally attempt to distil the most convincingly documented facts and ideas from the theoretical and empirical literature which I have reviewed.

ACKNOWLEDGMENTS

I WISH TO EXPRESS my gratitude and indebtedness to a number of teachers, colleagues and friends whose encouragement, advice and interest were very important to me in connection with this book: Dr. John C. Whitehorn, Professor of Psychiatry at Johns Hopkins, whose kindly and generous encouragement prompted the expansion of what was a brief paper into a full-length study; Dr. Kenneth E. Appel, Professor of Psychiatry at the University of Pennsylvania, who provided the impetus and the enthusiasm which eventually led to the publication of this manuscript.

I am especially grateful to Dr. Albert J. Stunkard of the University of Pennsylvania for his continuing interest and for his generously given encouragement, help and advice. His sensitive and thoughtful suggestions in matters of style, content and philosophy were invaluable to me.

I am also indebted to Dr. John Imboden of Johns Hopkins and to Dr. Frederick Ziegler, now of La Jolla, California, for their interest in reading large sections of the manuscript prior to its publication.

I wish to acknowledge a special debt to three friends who have helped to shape my thinking in psychiatry and whose influence is consequently woven into the structure of this book: Dr. Robert O. Jones of Dalhousie University, Halifax, Nova Scotia, who taught me an orientation to psychiatry that is, in its essentials, unchanged to this day; Dr. Eugene Meyer of Johns Hopkins with whom, for several years, there has been a continuing and stimulating exchange of ideas; Dr. Solomon Hirsch of Dalhousie University, with whom I have had so many long, exciting discussions about psychiatry and about life.

Finally, I am deeply grateful to Mrs. Betty Brewer for her patient and careful preparation of this manuscript. Her interest, forbearance and good humor were beyond the call of duty.

Acknowledgment is due to the editors of *The Bulletin of the Maritime Psychological Association* and *The British Journal of Medical Psychology* for material previously published and re-utilized in this book.

M.M.

CONTENTS

PSYCHOANALYTIC CONCEPTS OF DEPRESSION

Chapter I

1. INTRODUCTION

THIS PRESENT STUDY begins in the decade around the turn of the century. It was in this period that Kraepelin, Meyer and Freud began to develop the theories that in one way or another were destined to influence psychiatric thinking so decisively. Now, over sixty years since these workers first began to apply their integrative and intuitive genius to the understanding of human behavior, we are beginning to gain some insight into the reverberating depths of this complex problem.

One question that has always engrossed the attention of those who have studied the depressed states has been how the various kinds of depression are related to one another. It was Kraepelin's attempt to solve this riddle that ushered in the modern period of psychiatric thought. It was this enigma that preoccupied the German students of the problem for the first twenty-five years of this century, and the English clinical psychiatrists for the next twenty-five years. Nor will it fail to engage the attention of the present writer.

To appreciate the intellectual atmosphere in the psychiatric world of the eighteen nineties, the time when this study begins, it is worth while take note of the subjects which drew forth comment from Adolf Meyer, who was to do so much to revolutionize and humanize American psychiatry. In 1895, in *A Review of the Signs of Degeneration and of Methods of Registration,* although protesting against the psychiatric over-emphasis on what were known as the stigmata of degeneration, Meyer nevertheless conceded that the "alienist" could not dispense with such a study, and provided detailed suggestions for the observation and measurement of these

3

signs. For example, he advised that "for the study of facial asym-
metries the following oblique measures should be taken: Distance
from the external angle of the eye to the angle of the mouth-right;
left . . . etc." He listed twenty-two ear anomalies and included a
method of analysis of the parts of the ear which contained thirty-
four questions on each ear.

The climate of general psychiatric thought as late as 1916 is
suggested by the fact that in a discussion of the data on heredity,
Meyer pointed out that the concept of morbid taint, which had
come to preoccupy the psychiatric world, had become closely associated, in the profession's mind, with the concept of degeneration.
A morbid taint was considered by many workers to be fully
established when there was a "history of gout, rheumatism, diabetes,
gravel, phthisis, migraine, epilepsy, asthma, or of peculiarity of
character, criminal record, or nervous or mental disorders in one or
more persons of the family." In opposition to this loose thinking
he contended that no statements about heredity could be admitted
except "where the corpus delicti, the inherited feature, has a
sufficient relation to the disturbance of health which brings the
person under consideration."

In England in the eighteen nineties, so strongly did the psychiatric profession believe in the etiological role of heredity and
degeneracy in mental illness, that Henry Maudsley, the founder
of the famed London psychiatric teaching and research hospital,
could imply (1895) that it was useless to think about prognosis in
terms of the usual course of any particular clinical entity since
the real determining factor was the inexorable unfolding of each
individual's illness in accordance with his particular inherited
constitution.

In Germany, probably the two outstanding writers other than
Kraepelin were Wernicke and Ziehen. Wernicke, besides presenting
a mass of acutely observed empirical data, and influenced by his
brilliant demonstration of sensory aphasia, attempted to correlate
psychopathology and brain pathology far beyond where the facts
would allow — the kind of attempt that Meyer was to decry so
vehemently a little later. Ziehen was so interested in the derangements of psychological elements such as sensations, memories,
intellectual tones of feeling, etc. that this influenced his classifica-

tion of mental disorders. For example Meyer (1904a) pointed out in his chapter on paranoia that Ziehen placed "side by side the chronic incurable states of delusions of persecution and grandeur, lasting the entire life, and the acute curable exhaustive puerperal psychoses, delirium tremens, periodic and circular disorders, and even the transitory deliria of epileptics." As Kraepelin (1894) remarked, " 'We evidently stand here on the ground of hot and cold fevers, as they were spoken of before the days of stethoscope, thermometer, and pure culture.' "

2. KRAEPELIN AND MEYER

It was in this era of conflicting emphases on grossly misunderstood hereditary factors, isolated psychological components and overextended neuropathological speculations and in the period of the magnificent advances in the study of disease entities facilitated by "the stethoscope, thermometer and pure culture," that Kraepelin published the revolutionary fifth edition of his textbook in 1896. In an effort to define disease entities in psychiatry on the model of general paresis of the insane, with an etiology, a course and an outcome, Kraepelin broke away from contemporary thinking and gathered together from the four corners of the psychiatric world a number of previously separately designated symptom-complexes into two main divisions, the episodic non-deteriorating manic-depressive insanity and the progressive deteriorating dementia praecox.

Under the concept of manic-depressive insanity, Kraepelin included numerous disorders variously named and with previously ascribed very diverse outcomes, e.g., simple melancholia, melancholia with delusions, melancholia activa, periodic psychosis, simple mania, etc. In his words (quoted from Meyer, 1904b), "manic-depressive insanity comprehends on the one hand, the entire domain of so-called periodic and circular insanity, and on the other, simple mania usually distinguished from the above. In the course of years I have become more and more convinced that all the pictures mentioned are merely forms of one single disease process . . . . It is, as far as I can see, quite impossible to find any definite boundaries between the single disease pictures which have been kept apart so far. From 'simple' mania, the numerous cases with two, three, four attacks in a lifetime lead over quite gradually to periodic forms, and from these we reach circular insanity, through those cases in which a more and more marked initial or terminal stage of depression gradually complicates the pure picture of mania, or in which the long series of maniacal attacks is unexpectedly interrupted by a state of depression . . . . Manic-depressive insanity, as its name indicates, takes its course in single attacks, which either present the signs of so-called manic excitement (flight of ideas, exaltation, and over-activity), or those of a peculiar psychic depression with psycho-motor inhibition, or a mixture of the two states."

Thus its course. As for its outcome, he observed no essential deterioration (unlike dementia praecox) no matter how severe the individual attacks. With regard to etiological factors Kraepelin was uncertain. He (1902) postulated that "defective heredity is the most prominent, occurring in from seventy to eighty per cent of cases . . . Physical stigmata may also be present . . . Of external causes, besides gestation, alcoholic excesses are perhaps the most prominent; others are mental shock, deprivation, and acute diseases."

By the term "disease process" Kraepelin had no vague concept in mind. He meant an illness with a definite neuropathology but with the diversification of symptomatology mentioned above. What this anatomical pathology might be, he had no idea. But that it existed, he had no doubt. Bleuler, although Freudian in some ways was in this respect essentially Kraepelinian. What he said of schizophrenia (quoted in Meyer, 1908) he may well have said of manic-depressive insanity, "The real disease or disease process is still wholly unknown. It may be an auto-intoxication or an infection or anything whatsoever." And Nissl (1902) another follower of Kraepelin dogmatized as follows: " 'In almost all the functional psychoses it is possible to demonstrate anatomical findings in the cortex. As soon as we agree to see in all mental derangements the clinical expression of definite disease processes of the cortex, we remove the obstacle which today makes impossible all agreement among alienists.' "

Kraepelin's bold hypothesis gave rise to two major controversies that raged in German psychiatry for many years. From his original

concept of manic-depressive insanity he had excluded the melancholia of the involutional period which he considered a separate
clinical entity with variable prognosis. In this entity he included all
the morbid anxious depressions of the later years that did not
represent phases of other psychoses. This exclusion engendered
considerable controversy until Dreyfus (1907), following a study
of a series of melancholics at the Heidelberg Clinic, demonstrated
their almost universal eventual recovery except where dementia
intervened. Thus, by using Kraepelin's own criterion of prognosis
he contended that this syndrome belonged in the general category
of manic-depressive insanity. This evidence caused Kraepelin to
concede the point and in the eighth edition of his text, he accepted
the orphan child of involutional melancholia into the all embracing
entity of manic-depressive insanity. But this concession merely
provided more ammunition for a withering attack on the whole
concept of "disease entity" — clinically distinguishable "Krank-
heitseinheiten" — by such men as Hoche (1910) who trenchantly
pointed to the Kraepelinians as giving " 'the impression of a great
number of diligent workmen, most energetically engaged in clarifying a turbid fluid by pouring it busily from one vessel to another.' "
It was, he said, as if " 'a kind of thought compulsion, a logical and
aesthetic necessity, insists that we seek for well-defined, self-
contained disease-entities, but here as elsewhere, unfortunately,
our subjective need is no proof of the reality of that which we
desire, no proof that these pure types do, in point of fact, actually
occur.' "

And indeed the matter was not as simple as some of the sys-
tematizers had made it appear. Kraepelin taught that a sufficiently
careful scrutiny of the symptomatology of any patient should
provide the basis for a valid prognosis of whether he would or
would not deteriorate, i.e., whether he belonged in the manic-
depressive or the dementia praecox category. It sounded too good
to be true. And so it was. Even in Kraepelin's hands, in his own
clinic, it proved to be impossible only too often to prognosticate
correctly. Too many patients diagnosed as manic-depressive became
chronic and too many cases with apparent deterioration surprisingly seemed to recover. And there were many patients who
defied classification in either group. By 1920 even Kraepelin was

forced to concede that " 'we are thus obliged to limit to the utmost the assumption that this or that disorder is characteristic of a definite disease-process.' "

In the United States, Adolf Meyer gave Kraepelin's classification a very appreciative reception. In 1896, he introduced Kraepelin's scheme of diagnosis into the Worcester Hospital, probably the first institution outside of Kraepelin's own clinic in Heidelberg to make use of it. He felt that Kraepelin's new alignment of clinical pictures brought order into a previously hopelessly confused situation. And his emphasis on outcome appealed to Meyer's essentially human outlook. But by 1905, Meyer was warning against the over-extension of the terms manic-depressive and dementia praecox lest a new kind of arbitrary confusion be set up. He stressed the fact, for example, that there were many depressions which had neither the characteristics of manic-depressive depression or the involu-tional melancholic depression. And later on, he (1921) was to protest even more vigorously that "safer clinical methods should be used than the largely prognostic considerations of Kraepelin, and that dynamic formulations come closer to the needs of both physician and patient than the formal and peremptory dichotomy claimed by those who see but one of two fates, either manic-depressive disorder or dementia praecox." But by this time he had already formulated his psychobiological theory of reaction types — biological reactions of the mental type — and had definitely discarded the concept of disease entities, a concept of which, indeed, he had been suspicious from the very beginning.

By 1908, he had already become impatient with his colleagues' hypnotic preoccupation with undiscovered lesions in the cortex. "To try and explain a hysterical fit or a delusion system out of hypothetical cell alterations which we cannot reach or prove is at the present stage of histophysiology a gratuitous performance. To realize that such a reaction is a faulty response or substitution of an insufficient or protective or evasive or mutilated attempt at adjust-ment opens ways of inquiry in the direction of modifiable determin-ing factors and all of a sudden we find ourselves in a live field, in harmony with our instincts of action, of prevention, of modification, and of an understanding doing justice to a desire for directness instead of neurologizing tautology. The conditions which we meet in psychopathology are more or less abnormal reaction types, which we want to learn to distinguish from one another, trace to the situation or condition under which they arise, and study for their modifiability. . . . . Steering clear of useless puzzles liberates a mass of new energy."

It is interesting to speculate how much this early awareness of and interest in the reactive aspects of depression and other psychopathological formations was stimulated by Freud's early work in this field. Meyer was writing review articles on analytic theories as early as 1905. However, his interest in psychopathology took a significantly different form, manifesting itself in an investigation of the faulty reactions to life and of attempts at their modification rather than in the study of complexes and the unconscious.

Despite a prophetic observation of his that he had previously made ("any attempt at inventing too many new names meets a prompt revenge, as the fate of the books of Kahlbaum and Arndt have shown") Meyer (1904b) devised an entirely new Greek terminology based on the root word "ergasia" implying activity of the individual as a person. The affective reactions became known as the thymergasias and included the manic-depressive group of Kraepelin's together with the agitated depressions of the involutional period.

What had been accomplished in these hectic and fruitful years around the turn of the century? Not only new theories but actually new dimensions had been introduced into the study of behavior. By adding the dimension of time with his interest in the outcome, Kraepelin had been able to discern two main clinical pictures in the utterly confused mass of nineteenth century psychiatric functional disorders — clinical pictures which he boldly labelled disease processes. In the United States, this concept first met with appreciation and then with impatience and then finally in his pragmatic way Adolf Meyer became surfeited with the pointless devotion to an undemonstrated brain pathology, and encouraged by the Freudian stirrings across the water he helped to add another new dimension to psychiatry — the dimension of depth. Psychiatrists, under the influence of Meyer and of Freud were no longer to stand at a distance content to describe what they saw but were to inquire into what lay beneath the surface manifestations of psychopathology; in other words, to explore with increasing interest the depths of human personality. Psychiatry ceased to be a psychology of surfaces and became a psychology of depths. And this new interest in depth was to extend the interest in time from its exclusively forward glance backwards to the beginnings of habit deterioration and the crystallization of character structure. And thus, from its long history as a classificatory and descriptive science was psychiatry humanized in these few decades.

Yet, after all these years, one must agree with Lewin (1950) that despite the fact that Kraepelin's concepts were stripped of their universal usefulness, his careful subdivisions nullified, and the implications of an organic disease process not validated, "it must be something more than respect for authority that has kept us Kraepelinians tacitly, when we speak in psychiatric terms."

3. HOCH, KIRBY, AND OTHERS

During particularly the second decade of this century a series of thoughtful studies was published by a group of workers centered around the New York State Psychiatric Institute. Under the leadership of August Hoch, Kirby and McCurdy drew inspiration from three sources: Meyer's emphasis that psychiatric syndromes were biological types of reactions, Freud's observations on the unconscious and on infantile sexuality, and Kraepelin's interest in the outcome of disorders. Under the influence of Meyer and Freud they studied and corroborated the importance of psychological factors in the depressive reaction types. Their work seemed to promise much but actually accomplished little in the direction of a psychodynamic and psychogenetic understanding of depression. What was accomplished however as Lewin (1950) has pointed out, was that they helped to make American psychiatrists interested in the psychological aspects of depression and thus more receptive to psychoanalytic thought on this subject.

Sharing Kraepelin's interest in deterioration and recovery, they delineated several groups out of the amorphous mass of dementia praecox, which they considered to have a good prognosis. These included a carefully described group of stupors (Hoch, 1921) (called "benign stupors" by them) and perplexed states (Hoch and Kirby, 1919) which, because of their favorable prognoses, they labeled "benign psychoses" allied to or included in the manic-depressive group. Hoch attempted to prove that depression and elation were not the only two affect anomalies in this group, but that apathy, agitation and distressed perplexity also belonged there. "In other words," as MacCurdy (1921) commented, " 'anxiety-apathy Insanity' would be as appropriate, theoretically, as Kraepelin's term."

In 1909 Kirby reviewed Dreyfus's monogram on involutional melancholia and refused to accept his contention that this condition was really a sub-group of manic-depressive psychosis. His rejection of Dreyfus's views was mostly based on what he considered the inadequate diagnostic criteria which Dreyfus had employed for these two disorders. And in a challenging paper, Hoch and MacCurdy (1922) took issue with Dreyfus's contention that melancholics almost always got better. They demonstrated that in their series there were cases which did improve (which they labelled "benign psychoses of manic-depressive variety") and cases which did not improve (which they called "malignant psychoses clinically related to dementia praecox"). Thus on the basis of Kraepelin's criterion of prognosis, they disputed the unity of the involutional melancholic syndrome. In these days of improved therapeutic techniques we do not often observe the uninfluenced course of this disorder so it might be of interest to note that they considered a patient hopeless only if he failed to show improvement after four years. Their malignant cases were characterized by restriction of interest or affect (instead of e.g. the frank fear reactions in the benign cases), attention to the body of either a severe hypochondriacal nature or of an autoerotic type and by irritability or peevishness.

4. BLEULER AND THE EFFECTS OF HIS THEORY

It will have been observed that all this classification and study was mostly based on the criterion of recoverability. If the patient recovered, the illness was a benign psychosis and was most probably allied to manic-depressive insanity. If not, dementia praecox claimed him.

Although productive of much sound work and valuable observation this obsessive pre-occupation with prognosis was just about outliving its usefulness when Bleuler struck the blow that was destined—not immediately, it is true, but inexorably—to bring that phase of psychiatry to a close. In 1911 he published his descriptive and theoretical tour de force on schizophrenia and declared the problem of prognosis deceptive. It was his belief that the accepted standards for recovery were altogether too gross and he implied that many syndromes were said to have a good prognosis when actually some deterioration had taken place. He therefore contended that the diagnosis of a disorder be made by clinical symptomatology and specifically, as far as the so-called functional psychoses were concerned by the presence or absence of certain characteristic primary symptoms.

He devised the term "schizophrenia," by which he designated "a group of psychoses whose course is at times chronic, at times marked by intermittent attacks, and which can stop or retrograde at any stage, but does not permit a full restitutio ad integrum. The disease is characterized by a specific type of alteration of thinking, feeling, and relation to the external world which appears nowhere else in this particular fashion." And it was this "specific type of alteration," of which he gave numerous examples, that he considered diagnostic, not the outcome which was so difficult to estimate. He felt that the degree of failure to reach full recovery was sometimes so slight that to detect it taxed the observational powers of a skilled psychiatrist, but that it existed he considered implicit in his conception of the disease.

The "outcome" in the Kraepelinian sense was dethroned. The result of this new outlook, as far as the entity of manic-depressive psychosis was concerned, was that those cases of affective disorder which demonstrated contaminating schizophrenic signs were stripped away from it. Bleuler's criteria of diagnosis, if not his concept of the schizophrenic disease process, gradually met with acceptance throughout the American psychiatric world. The perplexed states are now considered to be unquestionably schizophrenic. And Rachlin, in a follow-up study of Hoch's benign stupor cases (1935) and in a later statistical study of this syndrome in five New York State hospitals (1937) revealed the schizophrenic nature of this so-called benign psychosis. So far did the criterion of deterioration prove irrelevant for the diagnosis of schizophrenia that the concept now includes what is variously termed "ambulatory schizophrenia"

(Zilboorg, 1941), "pseudoneurotic" forms of schizophrenia (Hoch and Polatin, 1949) and "borderline states" (Knight, 1953).

The disputable entity of involutional melancholia had been originally excluded by Kraepelin from his manic-depressive category on the basis of its poor prognosis. It had later gained entrance to this grouping after Dreyfus had defended its ultimately favorable outcome. Hoch had then shown it to have a variable prognosis and had therefore split it up into a benign and a malignant form. Now that prognosis had been discarded as a differentiating feature, it was re-established as an independent diagnostic entity, primarily as a the result of a series of papers the most significant of which were those of Titley (1936), Palmer and Sherman (1938) and Malamud, Sands and Malamud (1941). These papers, all based on the comparative study of involutional melancholic patients with manic-depressives, and also in Titley's paper with normal subjects can be summarized as arguing that involutional melancholia is an entity or syndrome different from manic-depressive psychosis in at least two areas, prepsychotic personality and symptomatology.

Prepsychotic manic-depressives are described by Henderson and Gillespie (1950) as having "frank, open personalities. They are either bright, talkative, optimistic, aggressive people, who make light of the ordinary affairs of life, or else they take a gloomy outlook, bewail the past, make mountains out of mole-hills; or there is a combination of the above moods, rendering the person emotionally unstable and variable." While differing in some details, this description, so reminiscent of similar descriptions by earlier writers, also characterizes the prepsychotic personalities of the manic-depressive patients whom Titley and Palmer and Sherman studied.

Contrasted with this picture is Noyes' (1948) impression of the prepsychotic personalities of involutional melancholics: "A review of the patient's previous personality and temperament often shows that he has been an inhibited type of individual with a tendency to be quiet, unobtrusive, serious, chronically worrisome, intolerant, reticent, sensitive, scrupulously honest, frugal, even penurious, stubborn, of stern unbending moral code, lacking in humor, overconscientious and given to self-punishment . . . . . often his interests have been narrow, his habits stereotyped, he has cared little for recreation, has avoided pleasure and has had but few close friends."

Titley's description is in the same vein. "Narrow range of interests, difficulty in adjusting to change, limited capacity for sociability and friendship, rigid adherence to a high ethical code, marked proclivity for saving, reserve that becomes positive reticence so far as intimate matters are concerned, an ever present anxious tone, profound stubbornness, overwhelming conscientiousness and strained meticulosity as to person and vocation are constant concomitants of the group." All of these writers were quite agreed that the involutional melancholics and the manic-depressives whom they studied differed markedly in their prepsychotic personalities.

As for the differences in clinical symptomatology, Henderson and Gillespie's observations also reflect the empirical findings of this group. They described the manic-depressive as being characterized by "difficulty in thinking, depression and psychomotor retardation" whereas in involutional melancholia there was "depression without retardation, anxiety, a feeling of unreality and hypochondriacal or nihilistic delusions." Palmer and Sherman stressed the agitation and the restlessness that they found in this type of patient and observed that in only three or four of their series of fifty involutional melancholics did they see definite psychomotor retardation.

It was also pointed out that while manic-depressives suffer many episodes of psychosis, the involutional patients fail to show a history of previous attacks of psychotic depression. Furthermore, it was argued that, unlike manic-depressives, involutional melancholics never have an episode of elation following their depression.

As a result of this preponderance of evidence and opinion involutional melancholia came to be considered a type of reaction which was essentially independent and different from manic-depressive psychosis, a point of view exemplified, for instance, in most modern text-books and in the Diagnostic Manual of the American Psychiatric Association (1952) where it is termed "Involutional psychotic reaction."

5. NEUROTIC DEPRESSIVE REACTIONS

It will have been noted that the concept of neurotic depression has so far not come up for consideration. Kraepelin had vaguely recognized such a condition which he included under the term congenital neurasthenia and which he listed under the category of

Constitutional Psychopathic States. He had also recognized that some depressive psychoses seemed to be precipitated by environmental factors. His pupils made similar observations, all characterized by a high degree of indefiniteness.

In the British literature, the controversy over whether there was any difference between neurotic and psychotic depressions was set off by a highly provocative and challenging paper in 1926 by Mapother, the head of the Maudsley hospital. His paper started off a debate that continued for years and led to an extensive clinical and theoretical study of the question. He asserted that "the distinction between what are termed neuroses and psychoses has really grown out of practical differences, particularly as regards certification and asylum treatment . . . . I can find no other basis for the distinction; neither insight, nor cooperation in treatment, nor susceptibility to psychotherapy will serve . . . . To assume that an enduring physical basis for habitually abnormal behaviour is probably non-existent because at present its exact nature is not demonstrable, seems to me a flat defiance of all relevant experience in medicine . . . . It is at least conceivable that some of the primary modes of abnormal mental reaction correspond to fairly definite bodily changes, perhaps to particular systems of neurons which we shall some day be able to identify." The heated controversy that followed, in addition to directing attention to the actual clinical study of depressed patients threw a good deal of light on the state of thinking in English psychiatric circles two decades after Meyer had propounded his views on psychological reactions.

Mapother's observations met with a resolute and sometimes acrimonious rebuttal. In order to prove that there was a difference between neurotic and psychotic depressions, appeals were made to differences in prognosis, heredity, body build, psychological and physical symptoms, dependence on or independence of external stimuli, metabolic factors and insight. Dissenting voices declared that manic-depressive psychosis "was an unalterable congenital component of the patient's entire being" (Strauss, 1930) whereas "reactive depression" was not endogenous and constitutional. There were some prepared to compromise, e.g., Reynell (1930) who felt that "complex entities cannot be classified into 'either-or,' they are usually both and sometimes neither. "

Impressed by the overabundance of views and paucity of facts, a number of observers turned to a scrutiny of their case material to determine whether they could delineate categories within the depressive group. Gillespie (1930) studied and was able to subdivide a group of twenty-five patients on the basis of their "reactivity." He did not use this term to refer to the psychological precipitation of the depression for he found that precipitating causes of a similar kind were almost universally present in his patients. By "reactivity" he meant "how (their) condition varied from day to day under the various external stimuli of general environment and treatment and the internal stimuli of their topics of pre-occupation."

In a comprehensive classical study of sixty-one depressed patients, Lewis (1934b) came to conclusions that directly contraverted the claims of the separatist school. He attempted to apply Gillespie's criterion of "reactivity" to each of his patients, and after a detailed discussion of the difficulties in applying this measuring rod concluded that the concept was so vague as to defy utilization. In order to come to some decision on the question of the role of environmental factors Lewis made an attempt "to decide with regard to each case whether there was a definite situational factor responsible for the precipitating or the maintenance of the symptoms. The criteria were the previous good health of the patient before this situation arose, the temporal relationship between the situation and the beginning of the illness, and the apparent adequacy of the situation from a 'common-sense' point of view. . . . . But the more one knew about the patient the harder this became . . . . (Except for ten patients) all the others were understandable examples of the interaction of organism and environment; it was impossible to say which of the factors was decidedly preponderant." As for the ten in whom there was apparent absence of psychogenesis or environmental influence, he concluded that the explanation may have been "our inability or disinclination to probe deeply into the total previous experience and reactions of the sick man." He observed that the better one knew a man's past, the more definitely did prodromal features become evident, and with reference to the precipitating factor acknowledged that "one does not call the last straw the cause of the camel's broken back, at any rate if one is talking in scientific language." And thus, after his comprehensive and scholarly study,

Lewis came to a conclusion that surprised no one who had properly understood the teachings of Meyer and Freud, namely that even in so-called endogenous psychoses, environmental factors and life-long patterns of reactions could be observed.

With regard to precipitating factors, Bellack (1952) recently summed the matter up as well as anyone. "In a differential consideration of reactive versus endogenous depression, one could actually speak of a continuum that extends from a minimum of an external precipitating factor to a maximum of such a factor. All other factors being equal, it can probably be said that the prognosis is better as the importance of external precipitating factors increases. What this very simply implies is that the patient who needed quite a realistic blow to react with a depression has a more stable premorbid personality than the one who reacted to a minimal situation; the first one would by the same token recover more quickly and more completely."

In 1940, Rogerson re-examined the problem of categorization. He rejected the criterion of environmental influence as a precipitating factor, which had over and over again been shown to be demonstrable in every type of depressive illness, and settled on a differentiation "concerned only with the patient's relationship to reality in a broad sense." Rogerson failed to work out the implications of this observation but nevertheless in his emphasis on the patient's clinical symptomatology, rather than on reactivity or prognosis, reformulated the problem in a manner that sharpened the issues.

In summarizing this prolonged controversy, we see that on the one hand, a group of writers, the outstanding ones among them being Mapother and Lewis, contended that there was no essential difference between neurotic and psychotic depressions, terms that were shown to be not synonymous with "reactive" and "endogenous" depressions. In support of their views, they pointed to similarities in precipitating factors, difficulties in clinical differentiation and they even speculated about a common physical basis for these disorders. This anti-separatist school gained a new exponent in 1952, when Ascher also questioned the value of the concept of neurotic depression, stating that in his opinion, "neither the course of the illness nor the therapeutic success of various procedures, nor

the danger of suicide are consistently dependent on" (this differentiation in diagnostic terms) "to justify their continued use."

On the other hand a group of workers, numbering among them
Gillespie and Rogerson maintained that there was an essential and
pertinent difference between neurotic and psychotic depressions.
The difficulty in distinguishing between these two clinical pictures
was variously assessed by members of this school. However their
stand has been implicitly supported by some work of a physiological nature which deserves mention at this point. Strongin and Hinsie (1939) found that parotid gland secretions were markedly decreased during the depressive phase of manic-depressive illnesses
but not in other types of depression. And Shagass and his co-
workers (1956) found that the sedation threshold ("an objective
determination based upon the EEG and speech changes induced
by intravenous amobarbital sodium") was markedly different in
patients with neurotic and psychotic depressions.

There is a third point of view which is best expressed in the literature by Tredgold (1941) and Bellak (1952). This maintains that
there is a continuum or graded series or spectrum at either end of
which the clinical pictures can be clearly and indisputably distinguished as neurotic or psychotic on the basis of symptomatology
(including the "relation to reality") but which contains a large
number of borderline cases which are admittedly difficult to clas-
sify.

Bellak tries to explain why one depressed patient is neurotic and
another psychotic by invoking the concept of "ego strength." By
this term he designates a "factor which by and large, determines the
form which the content assumes, how the content expresses itself—
as in a dream, a neurotic symptom, a delusion, or a hallucination."
He believes "that the . . . content may be hypothetically the same in
two patients, but that with a difference in ego strength, one patient
may be a neurotic (with neurotic symptoms) and the other may be
a psychotic (expressing the same content in delusions and hallucinations), while a third individual—a 'normal'—may express the
same content in dreams and in some character formations." However he is forced to admit that there are no reliable indicators of
ego strength.

Chapter II

1. ABRAHAM

DISREGARDING SOME EARLY tentative ideas of Freud's (1896), one might say that the psychoanalytical contributions to the subject of depression began with a paper by Abraham (1911). In this he declared that neurotic depression occurs when a person "has to give up his sexual aim without having obtained gratification. He feels himself unloved and incapable of loving, and therefore he despairs of his life and his future." He differentiated this from the mechanism in psychotic depression which he had studied in six cases of manic-depressive psychosis.

Freud (1909) had observed that in the obsessional neurotic, hatred and love were always interfering with one another. Abraham was struck by the presence of this ambivalent imbalance in the depressed patient too: "The tendency such a person has to adopt a hostile attitude to the external world is so great that his capacity for love is reduced to a minimum." In every one of his cases of psychotic depression, he concluded that the condition resulted from an attitude of hatred which was paralyzing the patient's capacity to love.

In a formula reminiscent of Freud's (1911) formulation for paranoia, Abraham explained the depression of such patients in terms of their use of the projective mechanism: " 'I cannot love people; I have to hate them.' " The content of this perception is repressed and projected externally, " 'People hate me . . . . because of my inborn defects. Therefore I am unhappy and depressed.' " Abraham felt that this repressed hostility revealed itself in dreams and symptomatic acts and particularly in a tendency to annoy other people and in violent desires for revenge.

He found that the more violent the patient's unconscious hostility, the more marked was his tendency to form delusional ideas of guilt; that is to say, he would feel just as guilty about his repressed impulses as if he had actually carried out his destructive and revengeful fantasies. And in this "omnipotence of thought" as Freud had called it, he also resembled the obsessional neurotic. Another symptom that Abraham explained on the basis of the strength of the hostile impulses in the depressive was the delusion of poverty which he so often observed. This feeling of impoverishment, he felt, sprang from a repressed perception by the patient of his own inability to love, that is to say, of his own emotional impoverishment. He also commented on the hidden pleasure the depressive seems to derive from his own suffering and from continually thinking about himself.

Abraham's next contribution to this problem was greatly influenced by Freud's views on infantile sexuality. In 1910, the latter had described several developmental stages or phases of sexual behavior prior to the genital stage. The phases were postulated on the basis of erogenous zones which were described as portions of skin or mucous membrane, the stimulation of which produced feelings of pleasure of a definite quality. In Freud's view the oral, or as he sometimes rather dramatically called it, the cannibalistic stage was the first pregenital phase of sexual organization. It was one in which the primary mode of sexual pleasure was the gratification of the oral erogenous zone, the mucous membrane of the mouth, by the act of sucking. Thus, sexual gratification was combined with the gratification of the need for nourishment. Freud postulated that later on in life the desire for sexual pleasure is usually separated from the desire for taking nourishment. One step on the way to this emancipation is the sucking of obects, e.g., the thumb, which though giving gratification to the oral zone does not satisfy the need for nourishment. The association of sexual pleasure with the lips and mouth is of course never completely broken but is integrated into normal sexual behavior as foreplay, as, for example, in the act of kissing.

In 1916 Abraham wrote a paper to corroborate and to supply clinical evidence for Freud's hypothesis of an oral pregenital stage of sexual life. It was mostly an empirical paper in which, from his clinical material, he recorded many examples of patients whose method of obtaining sexual pleasure had not achieved independence from the nutritive act.

First he mentioned the resistance that some children display to the act of weaning, and cited two examples: a girl of nine who could be induced to leave her bed in the morning only by being brought a bottle of warm milk and a boy of thirteen who had not yet been weaned from the bottle. He then described three adult patients who did not indulge in ordinary heterosexual activity but who did derive great pleasure from eating sweets. One of these patients, a female, in periods of abstinence from masturbation often experienced a violent longing for sweets. She bought and ate these sweets with great secrecy and with intense feelings of pleasure and gratification.

He repeated his earlier theory that lack of their accustomed sexual gratification leads to depression in many neurotics and went on to say that auto-eroticism in neurotics has two uses: to prevent a depression of spirits when it is threatened and to remove it when it has occurred. He included the various kinds of gratification of the oral zone among the auto-erotic methods used to dispel depression. He cites as an example a young female patient of his who used to relieve her depression by eating. Another patient of his, a male, lay in bed one day overcome with depression. His mother happened to bring him a cup of milk. "As he put the cup to his mouth and his lips came in contact with the fluid, he had, as he expressed it, 'a mingled sensation of warmth, softness, and sweetness.' This sensation surprised him, and yet seemed to be something known to him in the distant past; and at the same time it had an inexplicably soothing effect on him." Psychoanalysis and information from his parents revealed that he had had a very extended nursing period and an openly expressed desire for the breast lasting over several years. The cup of milk had presumably reactivated very early pleasurable memories and had served to alleviate his depression temporarily. Abraham also made passing reference to the frequently favorable effect on depressed neurotics of swallowing medicines, even when they had no pharmacological effect. He believed that in addition to the effect of suggestion, a bottle of medicine was useful in this way because of the accompanying gratification of the oral zone which awakened early pleasurable memories.

Abraham went on to consider two symptoms which were related to food and which appeared frequently in depressed patients, especially psychotic ones: the refusal to take food and the fear of dying of starvation. He had observed earlier that depressed patients mourn for their lost capacity to love. They then, he believed, regress to an earlier phase of sexual development in which gratification is obtained by oral means. In addition to, or instead of, the overt expressions of such a regression as were described above, Abraham postulated that in his unconscious the melancholically depressed patient directs upon his sexual object the wish to incorporate it. This incorporation is colored by the depressive's repressed hostility, so that really in the depth of his unconscious mind such a patient wishes to devour and demolish his object,* to destroy it by eating it up. He referred to the very revealing self-accusations of this type that one observes in such patients, and quoted an example from Kraepelin: " 'According to himself the patient had plunged the whole world into misfortune, had eaten his children and drunk up the springs of grace.' " In a later paper, he provided clinical examples from fantasies and dreams of the depressive's wish or tendency to incorporate and devour the beloved object. Abraham felt that only by keeping these unconscious cannibalistic wishes of the patient in mind, could one understand his refusal to take food. "He behaves as though complete abstention from food could alone keep him from carrying out his repressed impulses. At the same time he threatens himself with that punishment which is alone fitting for his unconscious cannibalistic drives—death by starvation."

Thus Abraham in these two papers stressed the importance of

---

*It is relevant at this point to refer to a reply made at a much later date by Fairbairn (1955) to a critic who complained that the term "object" was too impersonal and inappropriate a word to denote a person with whom a subject establishes a relationship. Fairbairn defended the usefulness of this comprehensive although clumsy term by pointing out that "whilst it is fundamentally with persons that the individual seeks to establish relations, the vicissitudes of emotional life . . . . lead to (relationships with) innumerable other objects which are not persons, and which may be either animate or inanimate. . . . . Apart from teddy-bears and the like (to which children become attached) . . . . there are also such concrete objects as totem-poles and such abstract objects as the State. It seems necessary, therefore, to have some comprehensive term to cover all these objects . . . ."

hostility and orality in depression. But he made this explicit reservation: "I have attempted only to explain the wish-content of certain depressive delusional ideas and the unconscious strivings that underlie certain characteristics in the conduct of the melancholic and not the causes of melancholic depression in general."

2. FREUD

In the following year there appeared Freud's classic paper *Mourning and Melancholia* (1917) in which he compared and contrasted melancholia with the normal emotion of grief. He cautioned that the various clinical forms which this disorder assumes, some of them appearing more somatic than psychogenic, do not seem to warrant reduction to a unity. He nevertheless ventured to define this state as follows: "The distinguishing mental features of melancholia are a profoundly painful dejection, abrogation of interest in the outside world, loss of capacity to love, inhibition of all activity, and a lowering of the self-regarding feelings to a degree that finds utterance in self-reproaches and self-revilings, and culminates in a delusional expectation of punishment." This description is essentially that of a psychotic depressive reaction. But from it we have no way of knowing whether he was referring, as Abraham explicitly was, to a manic-depressive psychosis or to the non-recurring depression of later life that clinical psychiatry calls involutional melancholia. From internal evidence in the rest of his paper, however, it seems quite clear that he too like Abraham was describing a manic-depressive melancholia.

Freud considered that melancholia resembled mourning in occurring after the "loss of a loved person or the loss of some abstraction which has taken the place of one, such as fatherland, liberty, an ideal, and so on," but he felt that unlike mourning, melancholia occurred only in specially predisposed people. The melancholic need not have lost his loved object in reality but may have lost it intrapsychically; that is to say, his emotional attachment to it may have been broken off unconsciously because of a hurt or disappointment. Also the patient may not be consciously aware of *what* it is that he has lost in the loved object, even when he can consciously perceive that a loss has occurred, and when he knows whom he has lost.

The normal person in mourning, Freud postulated, gradually and painfully withdrew his emotional attachment (his libidinal cathexis) from the loved object, i.e., from the intrapsychic representation of the loved person. To the grieving person, the world becomes poorer. But Freud noted that in melancholia it is the ego that becomes poor. It is his own ego that the melancholic vilifies and reproaches and hates. He does not complain of the loss of a loved object, but abases himself and laments his crimes and his inadequacies.

It was this self-directed rather than external reality-directed vilification that Freud found so puzzling. In pondering its meaning Freud conceded that the patient "was really as lacking in interest, as incapable of love" as he claimed; and that indeed there might be some truth hidden in his excesses of self-criticism. But "there can be no doubt that whoever holds and expresses to others such an opinion of himself . . . . that man is ill, whether he speaks the truth or is more or less unfair to himself." To understand this perplexing phenomenon Freud searched for an explanation beyond Abraham's view that the melancholic's self-reproaches were based on the projection of his lovelessness and hate.

Freud found such an explanation. "If one listens patiently," he wrote, "to the many and varied self-accusations of the melancholic, one cannot in the end avoid the impression that often the most violent of them are hardly at all applicable to the patient himself, but that with insignificant modifications, they do fit someone else, some person whom the patient loves, has loved or ought to love . . . . so we get the key to the clinical picture—by perceiving that the self-reproaches are reproaches against a loved object which have been shifted on to the patient's own ego. The woman who loudly pities her husband for being bound to such a poor creature as herself is really accusing her husband of being a poor creature in some sense or other." That is to say, instead of complaining, a patient is really accusing—and not actually himself but the person who was loved. "This kind of substitution of identification for object-love" represented for Freud "a regression from one type of object-choice to the primal narcissism . . . a regression from object cathexis to the still narcissistic oral phase of the libido." In Freud's developmental scheme the "oral" is, as we have seen, the earliest libidinal phase. In this phase the infant is presumed to be at first not able to distinguish himself from the world of objects. This lack of differentiation between the world and himself is referred to by Freud as "identification." The phase in which identification of this kind is said to exist is also referred to as "narcissistic" since it is presumed to be a period when all the libido remains invested in the ego and is not yet directed towards objects. The infant's mode of relating to the world at this time is alleged to consist largely of placing objects into his mouth and into himself as it were. This operation—"oral incorporation" or "oral introjection"—serves to enhance his presumed sense of identity with the object world around him.

It is in accordance with this developmental model that Freud considers melancholia to be a regression from object-choice to the earliest way of relating to objects, namely narcissistic identification, a type of relationship in which the object is not distinguished from the ego and in which all the libido is withdrawn from objects and invested again, as in the earliest phase of development, in the ego. The process by which this identification takes place is called, according to the infantile model, "introjection." Fenichel (1945) later referred to this as the "pathognomonic introjection" since the development of melancholia depended upon its having taken place. This concept of introjection as the important mechanism in melancholia was at variance with Abraham's view that it was projection that gave rise to depressive disorders and one does not again encounter this latter view in the literature.

Freud felt that this psychic introjection could only occur in that type of person whose object-choice was of a narcissistic kind. He thought that only an individual who loved persons who were very much like himself could so easily abandon his love-object and so readily confuse that object with himself. His feeling that only such people could develop melancholia was still, he very properly admitted, unconfirmed by investigation.

Freud postulated that after the loss of the object and its introjection, the hostile part of the ambivalence which had been felt towards the object manifested itself in the hatred and sadism which was directed at the ego (and its introjected object), in self-reproaches and self-vilification. In considering how the melancholia finally comes to an end, Freud theorized that "each single conflict of ambivalence, by disparaging the object, denigrating it, even as it were by slaying it, loosens the fixation of the libido to it."

Freud, as we have seen, in attempting to explain how the ego introjects the objects, postulated that it uses the method of oral incorporation, i.e., that it devours its object, and agreed with Abraham's explanation for the melancholic's refusal of nourishment. It seems to the writer pertinent at this point to quote a very significant warning of Blanco's (1941) (a warning that was to be repeated later in similar terms by Glover, 1945) that "it is very important to distinguish between a fantasy and a mechanism." This warning came much later in analytical history when the confusion between these two concepts had muddied English analytical thought to an extraordinary extent. Although still referring to the oral "method" of introjection, Lewin (1950) refers to various kinds of fantasies other than oral, which accompany the psychic process of introjection. He mentions cases in which introjection is conceived "as an introduction through the anus (Van Ophuijsen, 1920) as a smearing of feces into the skin (Lewin, 1930), as an inhalation (Fenichel, 1931), possibly as a 'taking in' by the eyes (Fenichel, 1937)." And recently Greenacre (1951) has also described a case of respiratory incorporation. Brierley (1941) in a very intelligent appeal for an awareness of the distinction between subjective and scientific descriptions of psychological events, also protests against mixing the language of fantasy with that of abstract terminology. She points out that "introjection" is the scientific term for a psychic mechanism whereas "incorporation" is a term which belongs to the realm of patients' fantasies.

It will have been noted that Freud did not concern himself with that aspect of the depressive's orality which manifests itself as the gratification of sexual needs by eating, drinking or sucking but that his emphasis was on the unconscious cannibalistic introjection of the loved object. In his description of what followed this psychic introjection, Freud referred to "the conflict between one part of the ego, and its self-criticizing faculty." In this, and in a similar remark in an earlier paper (1914), we have the germ of the idea that was to develop later into the concept of the superego.

Thus, from case material of psychotically depressed patients

Freud gave us these valuable ingenious intuitive formulations about the meanings of the melancholic's self-abasement and self-reproach. But as he himself was quick to protest, "Any claim to general validity for our conclusions shall be foregone at the outset."

One factor that caused him to refrain from generalizing too widely from his observations was his uncertainty about the extent of the constitutional or somatic component in melancholia. This reservation expressed itself several times in his paper. He made reference to the various clinical forms of melancholia "some of them suggesting somatic rather than psychogenic affections." He referred to the frequent improvement in the melancholic condition towards evening as being "probably due to a somatic factor." He considered that the marked ambivalence of the melancholic was "either constitutional" or a product of early experience. In his reluctance to indulge in premature generalization he raised the question "whether a loss in the ego apart from any object (a purely narcissistic wound to the ego) would suffice to produce the clinical picture of melancholia and whether an impoverishment of ego-libido directly due to toxins would not result in certain forms of disease."

It is of historical interest that, independently of Freud, an English worker, Alfred Carver (1921) made some very similar observations in his comments on the analysis of a case of melancholia. He came to the conclusion that it was after the loss of a beloved person that his patient lost her interest in the environment. Moreover, he felt that she unconsciously harbored a grudge against her husband for having died and left her. "The mental mechanism in the . . . . case seems to be a displacement of the reproach from the environment, including the husband, to the self; analysis showing the abuse which the patient heaped so lavishly upon herself was really intended for the former." He further spoke of "an identification of the self with a beloved person who is blamed for having caused the deprivation." He identified the mental mechanism in this case as introjection, and held that it was diametrically opposed to that of projection, "which is characteristic of the paranoiac."

In a footnote Carver remarked that since writing his paper, early in 1920, it had come to his attention that Freud, during the war, had also written on the subject of melancholia. From a review of this paper he judged that his own findings were not at variance with Freud's "unmeasurably though they must fall below them."

3. ABRAHAM

In his next contribution to the subject Abraham (1924) presented interesting clinical data to corroborate and to amplify Freud's observations. On the basis of the psychoanalysis of two manic-depressive patients and of brief glimpses into the structure of this illness in other patients, Abraham discussed further the relationship between obsessional neurosis and manic-depressive psychosis, leaning heavily on evidence obtained from his patients' libidinal and aggressive fantasies. He reiterated his observation that, like the obsessional neurotic, the manic-depressive is ambivalent to his love object, even in "free intervals" of relative health. And he also observed that in his free interval the manic-depressive resembles the obsessional patient in his character structure, e.g. in his attitude to cleanliness and order, in his obstinacy and defiance and in his feelings about money and possessions. He concluded that both of these conditions are related to one and the same phase of psychosexual development. But, he pointed out, these conditions are nevertheless not one and the same illness and he proceeded to outline his conception of the difference between them.

He stated that he did not know why sadistic impulses exhibited a special affinity for anal erotism, but that they did so appeared clear to him. He observed from empirical data that both anal erotism and sadistic impulses contain two opposite tendencies. Anal erotic gratification could be obtained in two ways; by the pleasurable excitation of the anal zone that accompanies either expulsion of feces or by the reverse process, its retention. Analogously, sadistic impulses contained two opposite tendencies: the tendency to destroy the object and the tendency to control it.

He postulated that in the anal stage of psycho-sexual development, an individual "regards the person who is the object of his desire as something over which he exercises ownership, and that he consequently treats that person in the same way as he does his earliest piece of private property, i.e., the contents of his body, his faeces." Thus a loss of an object is equated in the unconscious of such a person with the "expulsion of that object in the sense of a physical expulsion of faeces." Abraham drew attention to the "anal way" in which some neurotics react to every loss, i.e., with either constipation or diarrhea depending on whether in their unconscious they are denying or affirming the loss. He also cited the primitive ritual, described by Roheim, in which the deceased man's relaives perform the defecatory act on his newly made grave. And he provided fascinating linguistic examples of the close unconscious connection between losing and destroying, between the anal-expulsive tendency and the sadistic destructive tendency; that is, he showed that a loss may be unconsciously equated either with an expulsion or a destruction of the object. Similarly he illustrated how the tendencies to retain and to control the object combine and reinforce one another.

He felt that the more archaic and primitive of these two sets of tendencies are those that aim at the destruction and expulsion of the object; and that when the melancholic and obsessional are compared, it can be seen that the former has broken off his object relationship while the latter clings to his. This Abraham saw as the crucial difference between these two conditions. As soon as a threat to their possession of the object takes place both types of patients react violently. But the melancholic regresses to the anal expulsive-destructive phase and unconsciously destroys and rejects his object and becomes depressed. The retentive tendencies come to the aid of the obsessional and he maintains contact with his object. Once the object has been given up, Abraham believed that the melancholic may regress even beyond the earlier phases of the anal-sadistic level to the oral phase, e.g. in his cannibalistic fantasies. And when he recovers, Abraham postulated that he progresses to the retentive-controlling level of the anal phase at which he may be able to function fairly well like the obsessional neurotic.

Abraham presented case material to corroborate Freud's essentially intuitive grasp of introjection. For example, he cited the case of the daughter of a thief who repeatedly accused herself of being a thief. He also described several cases of mourning in which certain of the physical and psychological characteristics of the deceased loved person were taken on by the mourner; but he stressed the important differences between this process in mourning and in melancholia. The mourner has had a real loss, a death, and is endeavoring to compensate for his loss, of which moreover he is quite conscious. The melancholic is depressed over an unconscious psychic loss and in his ambivalence is overwhelmed by feelings of hostility which he has to deflect on to himself.

Abraham observed that in mourning, affectionate feelings for the loved object easily displace hostile ones but that in the melancholic, ambivalence is so marked that love and hate are always in conflict. "A 'frustration,' a disappointment from the side of the loved object, may at any time let loose a mighty wave of hatred which will sweep away his all too weakly-rooted feelings of love. Such a removal of the positive libidinal cathexes will have a most profound effect: it will lead to the giving up of the object." Melancholia will then ensue. The abandonment of the loved object is followed in an ever-expanding manner by a detachment of interest from every human being, from his profession, from his former interests, from the whole world. But unlike the schizophrenic who may appear indifferent to a similar withdrawal from reality, the melancholic complains of his loss.

In considering the problem of the method of introjection, Abraham described one patient who, in his desire to repossess the loved object which he had rejected in the typical melancholic way, had a compulsive fantasy of eating excrement. By means of this and other examples from his patients, Abraham provided what he considered clinical corroboration of Freud's hypothesis that introjection takes place by an oral mechanism.

Abraham reported numerous clinical observations of cravings, fantasies, symptoms and perversions that centered around the mouth and which he took to be evidence that patients who had lost their objects and had regressed to the anal-sadistic level of libidinal development continued to regress even beyond that stage, to the oral level. Fantasies of biting the breasts, penis, arm or other parts of the loved object, of cannibalism and necrophagia or reaction formations against these impulses, such as refusal to take nourishment or resistence against chewing, he interpreted as evidence of regression to an oral-sadistic level; whereas he took fantasies of suckling or the relief of depressive feelings by the drinking of warm milk as signs of regression to an early oral-sucking stage.

Abraham agreed with Freud's shrewd observation that far from acting with the humility that he professes, the melancholic gives trouble to everyone, takes offence readily and generally behaves as if he had been treated with great injustice. He pointed out that his so-called delusions of inferiority, besides being reproachfully directed against the introjected love-object, may actually represent him to be a very powerful and omnipotent monster of wickedness. He drew attention to the contempt and condescension that many of these patients display. And he discerningly noted the latent grandiosity that in so many manic-depressives awaits the manic state to manifest itself.

Abraham found all of the following factors to be essential in the psycho-genesis of melancholia. Each one by itself, he felt, might have contributed to the formation of some other psychological disorder:

1. Rather than admitting a direct tendency to inherit manic-depressive psychosis, Abraham postulated a constitutional and inherited over-accentuation of oral erotism. By this he meant an increased potentiality for experiencing pleasure in the oral zone.

2. A special fixation of psycho-sexual development at the oral level, as a result of the constitutional intensification of oral erotism, leading to excessive needs and consequently excessive frustrations connected with the acts of sucking, drinking, eating, kissing, etc.

3. Early and repeated childhood disappointments in love, as when a child shatteringly discovers that he is not his mother's favorite, or even worse, that he is not really loved by her at all.

4. The occurrence of a child's first important disappointment at an age before his oedipal wishes are resolved, i.e., while his desires for his mother's love and his rivalry with his father have not yet reached a compromise. Abraham postulated that in such a case there may occur a permanent association of his libidinal feelings with the hostile destructive wishes that hold sway over him at this time.

5. The repetition of the primary disappointment in later life.*

*Abraham believed that since all the melancholic's "subsequent disappointments derive their importance from being representations of his original one, the whole sum of his anger is ultimately directed against one single person—against the person, that is, whom he had been most fond of as a child and who had then ceased to occupy this position in his life." He went on to postulate that the melancholic's self-reproaches and self-criticisms were aimed not only at his abandoned love-object but were also directed "against that former object." He found that the melancholic's hostility towards his mother was, as a result of the early disappointment he had suffered at her hands, even greater and more pronounced than his hatred and jealousy of his father, a state of affairs which he considered quite different from that which was found in other conditions.

Thus, the study of an admittedly small number of manic-depressives led to the following conclusions: that melancholia occurs in an individual with an inherited over-accentuation of oral erotism and with a consequent fixation at the oral stage of psycho-sexual development who has suffered early disappointments in his love relationships and who has a subsequent repetition of these disappointments. These first disappointments were believed to be particularly pathogenic if they occurred before the oedipal conflicts were resolved, the person thereafter being even more likely to relate to his love objects in a highly ambivalent way. Such an individual on the occasion of a subsequent disappointment finds his love so overwhelmed by an upsurge of hate that he abandons the object as if it were feces and then introjects it into his own ego and becomes narcissistically identified with it. He then heaps reproaches upon himself, i.e., upon his introjected object, until finally a second expulsion takes place and he is free again. After reviewing this process, Blanco (1941) ingeniously remarked, "Judging from his description, it looks as though (Abraham) had the idea that melancholia was a kind of mental indigestion." And considering Abraham's preoccupation with the unconscious libidinal and aggressive activities of the gastro-intestinal tract, this does not seem like an irrelevant observation. He himself refers to the love-object going through "a process of psychological metabolism within the patient." He seems to have thought of the melancholic's love-object primarily as something to gratify the excessive pleasure needs of the oral zone, i.e., as something to be sucked perpetually and unprotestingly and to be retained and controlled in an anal way. If it failed to fulfill this role, he thought of it as being cannibalistically incorporated and then sadistically battered and assaulted until, having lost its attraction as a love-object it was disdainfully excreted and rejected.

4. RADO

In the meantime Freud had moved on from his interest in instinctual development to a consideration of the structure of the mind. In 1927, he published *The Ego and the Id* in which he set up his scheme of the mental apparatus. In this scheme, by an animistic conceit, the superego became the repository of ego ideals, the precipitate of parental standards and the embodiment of one's introjected or internalized objects, the parents. It was in the framework of these structural concepts that Rado (1928) made the next important theoretical contribution to the study of depression. He travelled further along the trail that had been blazed by Freud and Abraham although one misses in his paper the abundance of clinical illustrations that the earlier two writers had used to document their conclusions.

As we have seen, Abraham emphasized what he thought of as the melancholic's constitutional intensification of oral erotism leading to excessive frustrations. Rado conceptualized all of this in a more psychological fashion describing what he termed the depressive's "intensely strong craving for narcissistic gratification" and his tremendous "narcissistic intolerance." He discerned that the depressive is like a young child whose self-esteem is overwhelmingly dependent on the love, approval, regard and recognition of others. The healthier human being, as he grows up, is able to derive self-esteem from his own achievements and activity. But Rado saw the depressive as too greatly dependent for self-esteem on love and approval from without, on what has been called external narcissistic supplies, and with a correspondingly high intolerance for narcissistic deprivation, i.e., for trivial offences and disappointments that other more secure individuals can shrug off.

Because of this disproportionate dependence on love and affection, the person prone to depressive states vigorously seeks evidence of regard for himself from his friends and love-objects. As Rado succinctly commented, he is "most happy when living in an atmosphere permeated with libido." However Rado felt that once he has won a love-object, he treats such a person as a possession, domineeringly and autocratically. If the love object then withdraws his love, the patient reacts with hostile bitterness and with angry vehemence. This constitutes the rebellion which Rado postulated occurs before every depression and which he believed helps to explain the far from humble touchiness and trouble-making of the melancholic.

It is only when this rebellion fails, Rado believed, that recourse is taken to "a fresh weapon (the last weapon)" to win back love. The ego punishes itself, is full of remorse and begs for forgiveness. Rado described melancholia "as a great despairing cry for love."

But the stage on which this love scene is taking place is no longer the real world. It is no longer the lost love-object which is being courted. The ego has moved from reality to the psychic plane. And it is this move from reality that constitues the psychosis.

The love-object whom the patient has lost may be considered as the latest representative of the objects whose love he has been seeking all his life, the original prototypes of which were his parents. When a child does wrong and angers his parents, penance and punishment restore their love to him. Soon, deeds which could incur the parents' disapproval are being atoned for by the child himself with a feeling of guilt, without the intervention of parental punishment. That is to say, the reparation takes place on the psychic plane and his self-esteem is again raised, just as it would have been if his parents had bestowed their love upon him after a period of estrangement. He has, as it were, won the love of his parents, his internalized parents or his superego by the punishment that was intrapsychically administered, i.e., by his guilt. His ego becomes the object of aggression or punishment by his superego which is, at one and the same time, the internalization of both his judging and his loving parents. After the punishment, the ego is again reconciled to the superego. In slightly less animistic language, the guilt serves the purpose of gradually decreasing the tension between the ego and the superego. Thus the sequence, guilt, atonement and forgiveness.

It was Rado's thesis that the melancholic goes through the same sequence. But why the guilt? "He feels guilty because by his aggressive attitude he has himself to blame for the loss of the object." But how can this explanation be reconciled with Freud's dictum that it was the introjected object that was being attacked? Rado integrated this into his theory by observing that despite his guilt, the melancholic cannot entirely absolve the object from blame either; that is to say, despite his repentence and remorse he unconsciously feels that the love-object is to blame for having provoked the quarrel by "caprice, unreliability and spite." So, part of the aggression vented by the superego upon the ego is, as Freud observed, directed at the introjected object. But it must be noted that the object is not all bad, for the depressive had once had a relation of love with it. Rado postulated that in the supplication of the superego, the ego is trying to win back the love not only of the archetypical love objects but also of the latest love object, whose good qualities have been introjected into this source and origin of all love and affection. In Rado's words, "The 'good object' whose love the ego desires is introjected and incorporated in the superego. There, in accordance with the principle which . . . . governs the formation of this institution, it is endowed with the prescriptive right . . . . to be angry with the ego—indeed very angry. The 'bad object' has been split off from the object as a whole, to act, as it were, as 'whipping-boy.' It is incorporated in the ego and becomes the victim of the sadistic tendency now emanating from the superego."

As a result of this sequence of hatred, guilt, self-reproach and punishment, the introjected "bad object" is chastised and eventually destroyed leaving behind the good part of the object, indistinguishable from and now a part of the archetypical love object, the source of love and self-esteem. The ego now "heaves a sigh of relief and with every sign of blissful transport unites itself with the 'good object' which has been raised to the position of the superego." This "blissful transport" may vary all the way from normal self-esteem to the excesses of mania. Thus Rado saw the melancholic process as a love drama, as a grand attempt at reparation, but enacted in the wrong sphere, in the psychic plane between the anthropomorphized institutions of the mental apparatus rather than in relation to the object world. He postulated however that the restoration of self-esteem results from this psychological sequence.

Rado felt that the only difference between a neurotic depression and true melancholia is that in the former the external object is not given up, and the reparative struggle, the despairing cry for love, is directed towards the love-object in the real world and not only in the psychic sphere.

In summary, Rado felt that the melancholic is a person with intense narcissistic needs who, after the loss of the love-object, first rebels angrily and then tries to restore his self-esteem by a reproachful, remorseful punishment of his ego (which includes the introjected bad part of his object) by his superego, which plays the parts both of the punishing critical agency and the fount of love and affection which the patient is so earnestly beseeching.

Comparing Rado's views with those of his predecessors, we can see that in considering predispositional factors, he ignored the element of constitution and instead emphasized the psychological pre-disposition. He expanded the concept of narcissism, stressing the precarious self-esteem of the depressive and his craving and need for external narcissistic gratification. He saw another facet in the self-vilification of the melancholic, namely its function as an expiation undertaken in order to win back love, in every way analogous to the punishment that a child must endure for wrongdoing in order to win back his parents' affection. He extended the concept of orality in a manner which will be discussed below. Though not entirely overlooking it, he paid little attention to the unconscious "mechanism" of anal expulsion. And he differed slightly from his predecessors in considering the obsessional character of the melancholic in remission as a defense mechanism to drain off his aggressive impulses into social channels. Furthermore he made a decisive contribution to the psychoanalytic theory of depression by recasting this theory in the framework of the structural concepts that Freud had introduced in 1927.

5. GERO

In the years that followed, many papers appeared, e.g., by Helene Deutsch (1932), Zilboorg (1933), Peck (1939) and others, illustrating with clinical material one or more features that had been noted so discerningly by Abraham, Freud and Rado. These characteristics included the intense narcissistic cravings, the ambivalence, the introjection, the self-accusations and the unconscious oral and anal symbolism of the dreams and fantasies. Helene Deutsch, following in the footsteps of her predecessors but being even more explicit wondered about the universality of some of these features. Speaking of the process of introjection, she admitted that "whether this is true for all cases of melancholic depression one cannot say with complete certainty . . . . There are without a doubt cases of melancholic depression in which an unusual severity on the part of the superego is alone enough to cause it to rage sporadically and even periodically against the ego."

Gero, in 1936, outlined in a clear and instructive fashion the course of therapy in two cases of depression, bringing the consideration of this subject down from the heights of theoretical speculation to the relatively solid ground of therapeutic work. He confirmed many of the classical analytical observations in two patients who had what the author described as deep neurotic depressions bordering on melancholia. It is worthwhile presenting his psychodynamic formulations of these two patients in order to illustrate these theoretical considerations in a somewhat more concrete manner.

One patient was a female who had for years a continuously depressive state which occasionally deepened into a condition dangerously near melancholia, and which was not relieved by any manic features. She did not complain, but on the contrary tried to make light of her difficulties, was reserved and reticent and tried to be rigidly self-controlled. Her character structure, as this brief sketch would indicate, was essentially obsessional. Analysis revealed a person with exorbitant narcissistic demands who reacted to disappointment with hate and wild sadistic impulses which she attempted to ward off with her rigid self-control. The resulting stiffness and self-consciousness kept people at a distance and thus frustrated her even further. Gero obtained ample evidence of oral and anal sadistic fantasies, e.g. fantasies of savage feasting on bloody meat and defecating on the analyst's grave. The lack of fulfillment of her immoderate and urgent needs kept her continuously depressed. She had identified herself with her lost love-object and had erected this object, her father, within herself, e.g.,she had taken over his obsessional character structure, his taciturnity and reserve. Gero reported that "she said herself that her father was so much within her, his self so much absorbed by the identification, that she could scarcely imagine him as an independent personality." It is interesting that despite this identification, she did not heap reproaches upon herself and her introject in the characteristic melancholic way that Freud had described. Her sadism was controlled by her obsessional character structure. Gero's formula for her depression was "Nobody loves me whatever I do, nobody understands me, I am lonely and forsaken—as I was in my childhood"—a statement of grief rather than a reproach or an atonement or any other restitutive measure.

The study of his second patient is also interesting and instructive. Although very complex, it too revealed a person with infantile narcissistic longings for attention, friendliness and love, whose overwhelming needs were hidden by a facade of self-sacrifice, consideration of others and extremely high ego-ideals. He was a man in his thirties who had had periodic severe depressions since the age of fourteen when his father had died, relieved by slightly manic phases and by free intervals during which he was frightened, inhibited and excitable. This patient exhibited very clearly Rado's double intro-jection of the object into the superego and into the ego. His high ego-ideal and his immoderate demands upon himself (which screened his covetousness and infantile greed) were the result of a strong identification with his father; and his endless self-accusations were directed against both his parents. Although exceptionally strong, healthy and robust he complained that he felt old, weak, forgetful and sick like his remembered elderly and decrepit father. His self-torment too was used aggressively against his mother to whom he repeatedly complained that nobody could help him. His tremendous hatred and hostility were also manifested openly in violent scenes between himself and his mother and in outbursts of rage against the analyst. In this patient Gero was particularly able to observe the voluptuous pleasure in self-accusations and the sa-distic intention behind this masochistic manifestation. There were also numerous examples of oral fantasies and at the depths of his depression the patient would feel a ravenous hunger.

Thus in these two patients Gero was able to demonstrate clearly the underlying infantile narcissistic hunger, the intolerance of frus-tration and the introjection of the love-objects. In the one patient, due to the use of the obsessive character defense, this identification did not lead to self-accusations nor was the aggression directed in a masochistic fashion at others. In the second patient the ego-ideals supplied fuel for the self-torment which was used to bludgeon those around him. This patient was not obsessive and Gero disagreed with his predecessors about the universality of the obsessional character structure in depression.

In addition to supplying the literature with his detailed study of these two cases, which contained much interesting material besides that specifically mentioned above, Gero contributed a broadened interpretation of the concept of "orality." Rado had postulated that the pleasurable stimulation that the infant experienced during feed-ing was not confined to the oral zone but culminated during the period of satiation in an "alimentary orgasm," a questionably useful term obviously used to underscore the libidinal aspect of the whole nutritive process. With fuller understanding of the significance of object relationships, Gero was able to point out that the importance of the "oral" experience in infancy had infinitely less to do with the satisfaction of the erotism of the oral or alimentary zones than with the wider and more comprehensive aspects of the mother-child relationship. "The essentially oral pleasure is only one factor in the experience satisfying the infant's need for warmth, touch, love and care." This of course conforms to the current usage of the term "orality" which has come to be pretty generally used in this symbolic sense, as the longing for "shelter and love and for the warmth of the mother's protecting body" rather than, or in some cases in addition to, the desire for pleasurable stimulation of the oral zone. It was in this very symbolic sense that Gero agreed with Rado and indirectly with his predecessors when he said that "oral erotism is the favorite fixation point in the depressive."

Gero asked why it was that the depressive persisted in his infantile demands for love and why he could not develop more ego-syntonic and mature ways of acquiring narcissistic supplies. This happened, he felt "because the way to genital love-activity is barred. In a genital love-relationship the infantile wishes for warmth and tenderness may also be fulfilled. Such a love-relationship is the only possibility for the adult to safeguard the inheritance of infancy. People for whom this path is not open—and they are the neurotics —suffer from an insoluble contradiction; for they long for something unattainable, being grown up they want to be loved like children. In other words the anxieties overshadowing the genital sexuality press the libido back into the pregenital positions. Thus these demands gain an uncanny force."

And from where do these genital anxieties arise? Gero, in the classical tradition, affirmed that they originate in the oedipal period. At that time because of excessively traumatic experiences, genitality and sexual fantasies become colored by aggression and guilt. "The neurosis ends when one has succeeded in mastering the genital anxieties, the feeling of guilt oppressing the genital impulses, and when the capacity of experiencing genital life and object-relations to the full, and without ambivalence, is re-established." Gero was able to show how genitality had been repressed in each of his patients because of its admixture with aggression and suffering and guilt. And he was able to demonstrate that after the specific character defenses of the patients had been loosened sufficiently for the analysis and the solution of the pre-genital fixations to take place, that the genital impulses with their accompanying anxieties could then be experienced by the patients and eventually, with the help of the analyst, mastered.

It is worth noting tht Gero's very detailed case studies provided no clinical confirmation of Rado's theory of intrapsychic propitiation in depression. Although he quoted Rado extensively he made no specific mention of this concept and one is forced to conclude that he did not find it demonstrated in his patients.

6. MELANIE KLEIN

The authors considered above regarded depression as one of the psychopathological disorders, a little more common than some others perhaps, but essentially of no more central importance than, say, the phobic states. It remained for the English writers to re-examine the implications of this complex of depressive feelings and anxieties and to discern and to emphasize its broader theoretical importance. They, as a consequence of their increased interest in this subject, provided the literature with perceptive appraisals and sensitive word-pictures of the depressive and allied conditions. They isolated theoretically and described clinically the painful torment of the state which they called the "depressive position."

Melanie Klein (1932, 1948) was the founder of the so-called English school and remains its most influential member. It was her contribution to psychoanalysis to push the area of analytical interest back to the infant's first year of life and to examine the effects of the processes of introjection and projection on his psychic development. It will be remembered that Freud, in his paper on melancholia, described the process of introjection as one of the essential features in the melancholic process. To judge by the examples that he and Abraham gave, this term implied the taking-on by the patient of some attribute of the lost love-object, either psychological or physical. Freud at first felt that this process occurred only when the object choice was of a narcissistic type. He later became aware that this process had wider significance than he had originally attributed to it. By the time he wrote *The Ego and the Id* (1923) he had come to see that introjection, the exact nature of which, he admitted, was still unknown to him "has a great share in determining the form taken on by the ego and that it contributes materially towards building up what is called its 'character.' " He felt that whenever an object is given up, it is reinstated psychologically within the ego and thus becomes part of the person. He even speculated about whether this identification might be the sole condition under which love-objects can be given up. At any rate, he felt that in the early phases of development this process is a very frequent one. In a classic dictum, he maintained "that the character of the ego is a precipitate of abandoned object-cathexes and that it contains a record of past object-choices." Thus introjection was conceived as occurring not only in melancholia but also whenever an object is lost, preeminently when the oedipal love objects are given up, in which case the resulting introjection gives rise to the formation of the superego.

Melanie Klein conceived of the process of introjection as occurring even in the first months of life. To present her views intelligibly in a concise form is always a difficult undertaking. Her theories often appear to be written in a strange dialect of the psychoanalytical tongue which has to be translated into the more standard speech in order to be understood. Her views have met with strong opposition on theoretical and clinical grounds and even her sympathizers (e.g., Blanco, 1941) have been driven to protest against "a certain number of developments in the Melanie Klein school, reminiscent of the casuistry of the Middle Ages. The introjected object has become something so concrete, so well delimited or sharply defined, that when one hears of people introjecting either the whole or part object, and then projecting it on to the outside world, introjecting it again, cutting it to pieces, blowing it up, putting the pieces together again—when one hears all this one cannot help recalling the animistic conceptions of children and primitive people." Nevertheless, despite what most American and many English writers consider her theoretical excesses and unjustified retroactive application of observable data, her observations on depressives are worthy of consideration and are helpful in the understanding of these patients.

In her use of Freud's and Abraham's concepts of oral, urethral, anal and other types of sadism, Melanie Klein (1932) examined these phenomena under the magnifying glass of her interpretive technique and transformed these sufficiently cruel-sounding concepts into phases of incredible savagery and hatred that are presumed to take place during the first year of life. She made her observations of the infant's sadism mostly from "derivatives of its phantasies . . . . for normally we only get comparatively faint indications of the small child's impulses to destroy its object." She pointed out, moreover, "that the extravagant phantasies which arise in a very early stage of its development never become conscious at all."

Her pictures of the sadistic fantasies during the first year, whether oral in type, in which the child gets possession of the mother's breast and the inside of her body by sucking, scooping, biting and devouring it, or urethral in nature with "phantasies of flooding, drowning, soaking, burning and poisoning by means of enormous quantities of urine" leave no doubt regarding her feelings about the vividness and imagery and strength of the aggressive drive during the first year.

Melanie Klein maintains that an infant reacts to frustration and to lack of gratification with rage and sadistic fantasies corresponding to his phase of development. When suffused with anger, an adult may feel several different anxieties as a consequence of his rage. He may feel anxiety about the very force of his anger, perhaps about the potential physiological harm to himself as a result of it. He may experience anxiety about the weakening of the emotional ties during the attack of rage, with the resulting feeling of being bereft of a loved object. He may also be anxious about retaliation and revenge from the object. An infant feels these same anxieties in the situation of rage even more intensely, according to Klein. She believes that the weakness of the infantile ego gives rise to a feeling of helplessness in the face of these immense tensions and to a state of fear of being exterminated by these powerful impulses, i.e., his rage constitutes an internal instinctual danger. In this danger situation mechanisms of defense are mobilized and some of this rage is projected outward to the object which, in the first few months, is a part-object, e.g., a breast. The danger, which is now felt to emanate from external persecutors as well as internal instinctual forces, influences the fantasied defensive sadistic attack on the mother's body.

These external persecutors are now introjected; that is to say, the child has fears of the external objects even when they are not present, and distorts the danger when they are present. This is the famous persecutory or paranoid position that is so important in Melanie Klein's theories: a phase of development in which the child is beset by anxieties about its own dangerous aggressive impulses and by anxieties about "bad objects" outside.

These nameless and formless fears may a little later assume more definite shape. Klein remarks that "in analyzing some quite young children I have found that when they are alone, especially at night, the feeling they had of being surrounded by all sorts of persecutors like sorcerers, witches, devils, phantastic forms and animals and their anxiety in regard to these had a paranoid character." Later these fears may be even further objectified in the form of animal phobias, according to Klein.

But to go on with how all this affects her views on depression (1934, 1940), she believes that it is not only feelings of hostility that the infant entertains towards his parent. Warmer emotional ties also exist when his needs are satisfied and when he is looked after. Gradually a feeling of being loved takes form and tempers the savagery and force of the early sadism; that is, in Melanie Klein's language, "good objects" are also being introjected. Another way of saying this is that the "good" loving *aspects* of the mother are introjected. These are experienced in the unconscious as "good *objects*." However, she maintains that until the infant can become confident of love despite his rage, every frustration, every removal of the breast, every absence of the mother is interpreted by him as a loss of the good object, a loss which is due to his own destructive fantasies and which is accompanied by feelings of sadness, guilt, and regret. She believes that this feeling of loss and sorrow can occur only when the warmth of a relationship with a loving "whole" person has once been experienced, and that this cannot happen as long as the relationship is purely on the level of need and satisfaction of that need by a "part object", the breast. "Not until the object is loved *as a whole* can its loss be felt as a whole." This is presumed to occur when "the ego becomes more fully organized."

Melanie Klein maintains that every infant regularly experiences these feelings until he becomes more fully assured of his mother's love for him, i.e., until he has firmly established his good objects within himself. Those children who are so unfortunate as not to meet with sufficient love for this to happen or whose reality testing is insufficiently developed to disprove these anxieties, who have never succeeded in securely installing their good objects within themselves and who consequently never feel sufficiently loved, are presumed by her to be always predisposed to return to the depressive position, to feelings of loss and sorrow and guilt and lack of self-esteem. In other words, they are particularly liable to depressive episodes.

The sorrow and desolation over the loss of the good objects (i.e., over the loss of all love, goodness and security) which she believes that every infant experiences periodically until his good objects are secured within himself (i.e., until, under the influences of his parents' love, he feels secure even when they are absent) is considered by her to be so overwhelmingly painful that it is accorded the rank of the central anxiety situation in human development, "the deepest source of the painful conflicts . . . . in the child's relation to people in general."

She calls this anxiety situation "the depressive position" and includes in it two sets of feelings: on the one hand, persecutory fears stemming from the dangers of internal aggressive drives and on the other, "feelings of sorrow for the loved objects, the fear of losing them and the longing to regain them."

Melanie Klein considers that while the infant is still in the depressive position he can not be certain that his good object has not been destroyed and lost to him forever when it becomes rejecting or denying. He still has not enough confidence in his own goodness and in the trustworthiness of the object to be sure that when this object denies him something that this rejection is only temporary or that when the object leaves him that it will return. His awareness therefore that his good object can unaccountably turn bad and his fear that it might at any time become lost to him— perhaps forever—are considered by Melanie Klein to be sources of pain and suffering to the infant. This liability to depressive anxiety and suffering is presumed by her to continue until his love for his real and internalized objects and his trust in them become securely established. Until this happens Melanie Klein believes that he has to resort to various defensive techniques in order to reduce his suffering and pain.

One of these defensive mechanisms is to deny his anxiety-creating awareness of the complexity of the love-object. It becomes for him at any given time either all good or all bad. When it is bad his depressive anxieties are confirmed. But by means of this defense he need no longer be aware that his good object can turn into a hateful and denying one.

As Mabel Blake Cohen and her colleagues (1954) were to emphasize later, this tendency to see objects as bad or good, black or white remains a striking characteristic of the adult manic-depressive who has presumably never successfully passed through the depressive position and who therefore has to resort to this and other defensive techniques to control his depressive anxieties.

Joan Riviere (1936) has drawn a vivid and almost poetic picture of what she presumes the underlying fantasy content of the depressive position to be: "the situation in which all one's loved ones *within* are dead and destroyed, all goodness is dispersed, lost, in fragments, wasted and scattered to the winds; nothing is left *within* but utter desolation. Love brings sorrow and sorrow brings guilt; the intolerable tension mounts, there is no escape, one is utterly alone, there is no one to share or help. Love must die because love is dead. Besides there would be no one to feed one, and no one whom one could feed, and no food in the world. And more, there would still be magic power in the underlying persecutors who can never be exterminated—the ghosts. Death would instantly ensue—and one would choose to die by one's own hand before such a position could be realized."

Although Melanie Klein (1934) speaks of little children passing through anxiety-situations, "the content of which is comparable to that of the psychoses of adults" it must not be thought, and she specifically disclaims this implication, that infantile psychotic states or phases are postulated. In differentiating what takes place in the child from what occurs in the psychoses of adults, she refers to the fact that in the child these psychotic anxieties never solely predominate but are quickly followed by and alternate with normal attitudes. But there are children in whom this quick changeover does not take place and in whom the depressive picture persists. Rene Spitz (1946) has graphically described "anaclitic depressions" in infancy following upon the loss of the mother. But it would appear that he is attacking a straw man when he denies that such depressed states are the lot of every infant. What Melanie Klein describes are not persisting clinical states of depression but the transient anxieties and the presumed content of the fantasies, essentially unconscious, of all infants.

It will be useful at this point to compare the views of the general analytic writers with those of Melanie Klein. As a general statement it might be said that the former occupied themselves with the concept of depression as a reparative mechanism, as a restitutive measure designed to overcome the psychic injury resulting from the loss of the object. Freud saw melancholia as a continuing period of torment during which the introjected object is punished for its badness until it is sufficiently devalued for the affective wounds resulting from its loss to disappear. Abraham described this process in greater theoretical detail but essentially from the same point of view. Rado expanded the concept of restitution and conceived not only of the introjected object being punished but on another plane of the patient repeating the archetypical pattern of suffering punishment himself in order to win back the love of his internalized love objects.

Melanie Klein, by way of contrast, became interested not primarily in the mechanism of reparation but in the factors that predisposed to depression and in the feelings and the fantasy content of the depressive state. Not that the other analysts had neglected this topic. Freud and Abraham had also speculated about the predisposition to depression. But it was Melanie Klein who first elaborated the theory that this predisposition does not necessarily depend on one or a series of traumatic incidents or disappointments but rather on the quality of the mother-child relationship in the first year of life. If this is of a type which does not promote in the child a feeling that he is secure and good and beloved he is, according to Melanie Klein, never able to overcome his pronounced ambivalence towards his love-objects and he is forever prone to depressive breakdowns. The predisposition to depression then is not necessarily characterized by specific traumatic events or overwhelming disappointments but is simply the result of the child's failure to overcome his early depressive fears and anxieties and his lack of success in establishing an optimal level of self-esteem. This outcome, according to Melanie Klein, depends in part on the prevailing attitude of the mother towards the child which is so important in determining how he comes to terms with his own ambivalence and with his guilty fears and sorrowful anxieties. Despite her numerous questionable premises then, Melanie Klein's basic contribution to the theory of depression consists of the concept of the "depressive position," a developmental phase during which the child has to learn how to modify his ambivalence and how to retain his self-esteem despite periodic losses of the "good mother."

Chapter III

1. INTRODUCTION

SEVERAL OF THE most important recent contributions have been concerned with the question of whether or not all depressive conditions have similar origins and similar mechanisms. Before discussing these issues it will be necessary to take up again for a moment the wearisome controversy concerning the difference between neurotic and psychotic and between "reactive" and "endogenous" depressions. It may be a bit surprising in view of the intensity of the debate in the clinical psychiatric literature that there is an almost complete unanimity on this issue among psychoanalytic writers. Practically every writer on this subject from Abraham and Freud onwards has explicitly or implicitly acknowledged a distinction between neurotic and psychotic depressive reactions. The criteria that have been used have been based neither on outcome nor on psychogenesis but rather on clinical grounds, that is to say, on symptomatology, on the extent to which the patient has withdrawn from or broken with reality.

It must not be thought however that analytic writers see this "turning away from reality" as a sharp end point or as an unequivocally recognizable element serving to distinguish, as it were, the neurotic sheep from the psychotic goats. Rado (1928) for example felt that neurotic depressions also involve a turning away from reality with the love object being replaced by psychic institutions and with the attempts to win back this love object taking place partly on the intrapsychic plane rather than in the external world. The word "partly" defines his view of the neurotic depression. The object is not really abandoned and the relation to reality is, despite everything, preserved. "It is only that the patient's hold on it is loosened and the weakly ego has begun to give up the struggle with the world. Thus, neurotic depression is a kind of partial melancholia of the (neurotic) ego; the further the depressive process extends within that ego at the cost of its relations to the object and to reality, the more does the condition of narcissistic neurosis approximate to melancholia."

In the same vein Fenichel (1945) wrote: "The difference between a neurotic and a psychotic depression . . . is determined by the depth of the narcissistic regression", by which he meant the extent to which "object relationships are replaced by relations within the personality."

It should be noted that it was Fenichel who first indicated quite explicitly what was certainly implicitly contained in Freud's and Rado's formulations but which had not previously been outlined so clearly. This was that in depression there were really two regressive processes taking place, an "instinctual" regression and a regression of the ego, processes which had previously somehow been telescoped together and thought of practically synonymously as an "oral narcissistic regression." Fenichel postulated that there was a regression to the oral phase of libidinal development in both the neurotic and the psychotic depression but that the latter was also characterized by the regression of the ego to the state before the successful establishment of a separate ego. He, like Rado, believed that all depressions represented struggles to reestablish self-esteem, but he felt that in a psychotic depression there was a regression of the ego to a period before it could be aware of objects as separate from the self. He did not wish to be understood as implying that the depressive psychosis was identical with this archaic ego state. "All psychoses contain elements that do not represent the repetition of infantile factors but remainders of the prepsychotic adult personality." Nevertheless he did mean that in a psychotic depression, the patient was unable to distinguish the object from himself.

This is what Freud (1917) had referred to when he had described the "regression from object-cathexis to the still narcissistic oral phase of the libido." It was in this sense but with his refinement of conceptualization that Fenichel defined the difference between a neurotic and a psychotic depression as "determined by the depth of the narcissistic regression," by which he meant the extent to which the object is given up and confused with the self, for he believed that in all depressions, neurotic or otherwise, identification *to some extent* takes the place of object relationships. And it is also in this sense and by the symptomatology that characterizes this regressive process that modern psychoanalytic writers distinguish neurotic from psychotic depressions.

As for the distinction between "reactive" and "endogenous" depression, it was Fenichel also who met this issue most squarely. He refused to be impressed by the seeming absence of precipitating factors in many a case of depression, believing that this argument overlooked the existence of the unconscious. He held that one does not distinguish between "endogenous" and "reactive" hysterical seizures on the basis of the absence or presence of immediate precipitating events because it is assumed that the apparently spontaneous attacks have unconscious precipitating causes. The same, he believed, holds true for depressions. He felt that every depression is to some extent reactive even though the provocation may not be demonstrable. "A person predisposed to illness by oral and early ego fixation may fall ill as a result of mild precipitating circumstances that are not readily observable; however, even one with relatively little predisposition may fall ill if severe and obvious circumstances appear."

Having observed that analytic writers did recognize a distinction between neurotic and psychotic types of depression, it might well be asked what the clinical basis was for the various assumptions regarding the specificity or universality of depressive mechanisms and depressive etiology. And it might be asked whether there is any evidence that these conclusions were based on clearly differentiated clinical material, and whether there is any consensus in the literature concerning the various aspects of depression. A glance at the literature is instructive.

It will be remembered that from the study of a small series of patients with manic-depressive psychosis, the correct diagnosis of which he took pains to establish, Abraham (1911, 1916, 1924) drew certain conclusions about the oral and anal fixations and fantasies found in this condition, made certain observations about the importance of ambivalence in the predisposition to this psychosis, and introduced the valuable concept of a "primal depression" in the infancy of patients with this disorder.

It will also be recalled that Freud (1917), after a careful study of the self-accusatory reproaches and delusions of manic-depressive patients formulated his theory about the introjection of abandoned loved objects in melancholia, protesting however that "any claim to general validity for our conclusions shall be foregone at the outset." So far from claiming general validity for his theory was he that he speculated "whether a loss in the ego apart from any object (a purely narcissistic wound to the ego) would suffice to produce the clinical picture of melancholia and whether an impoverishment of ego-libido directly due to toxins would not result in certain forms of the disease."

Rado (1928), as was seen above, on the basis of his experience but without producing any clinical documentation of his thesis postulated that there was only a quantitative difference between the neurotic and the psychotic depression and attributed general validity to the conclusions which Abraham and Freud had drawn so painstakingly from the study of fantasies, delusions and self-accusations in manic-depressive patients.

Later, Helene Deutsch (1932) was to be more reserved about the universality of the features and mechanisms which had previously been described. Speaking of the process of introjection, she admitted that "whether this is true for all cases of melancholic depression one cannot say with complete certainty . . . . There are without a doubt cases of melancholic depression in which an unusual severity on the part of the superego is alone enough to cause it to rage sporadically and even periodically against the ego." And Gero in 1936 disagreed with previous writers about the universality of the obsessional character structure in depressed patients.

By 1951 Rado had sufficiently lost his earlier certainty about the general validity of the classical psychodynamic formulation to remark, "We encounter depressions in drug-dependent patients, neurotics, schizophrenics, general paretics, patients afflicted with severe physical illness, etc. The question arises whether or not significant psychodynamic differences exist between depressive spells that occur in different pathogenic contexts. Further psychoanalytic investigation may provide an answer to this question."

Indeed it was a very pertinent question. Whether the formulations chiefly derived from the study of a small group of manic-depressive patients are as applicable to the wildly agitated depressive psychoses of the involutional period, the empty, lonely depressed conditions found in young schizophrenics and the listless apathetic post-viral depressions as they are to the deeply retarded periodic melancholias of the manic-depressive type is a very pertinent inquiry. It was a question which many workers had tended to ignore or to answer with misplaced and unwarranted confidence.

Gero (1953) addressed himself to this same question. He uttered a warning about the dangers inherent in not clearly recognizing the nature of the clinical material forming the basis of any particular theory. He pointed out that "we do not always realize that we are talking about different phenomena and arrive at theories which contradict each other." He not only believed that all depressed patients do not necessarily belong to the same clinical groups which Freud and Abraham studied, but he also felt that even "in the same type of depression different aspects of the symptomatology necessitate different explanations." He described a case of anorexia which showed many of the essential features of chronic depression but which nevertheless exhibited certain differences in symptomatology which he believed were indicative of different mechanisms at work in the patient. He felt "that such an approach reflects the general state of psychoanalytic thinking in our days. We are much less apt to reach easy generalizations, but much more able to develop concepts and correlations which are descriptive of the unending varieties of the phenomena presented to us by our patients."

2. BIBRING

Two writers, Bibring and Edith Jacobson have attempted to modify the theory of depression to take into consideration these challenging facts and observations. Of the two, Bibring's view (1953) although more simply written and more easily presented in a review like this, departs more radically, in certain respects, from the classical theory.

Bibring allied himself with those writers who see the depressive reaction as essentially an affective state characterized by a lack of self-esteem. Rado and Fenichel in particular had emphasized the loss of self-esteem in depression. Bibring agreed with them that the predisposition to depression is a result of traumatic experiences which occur in early childhood and which bring about a fixation to the state of helplessness and powerlessness.

But from here on Bibring struck out in a new direction. Previous writers had emphasized the "oral fixation" of the depressive. Fenichel, (1945), for example, speaking of traumata in early childhood stated that "the narcissistic injury may create a depressive predisposition because it occurs early enough to be met by an orally oriented ego." This meant that a failure to obtain love at a period in childhood when one's "lovability" and worth and self-esteem had not yet been decisively established left one chronically hungry for affection and filled with needs and demands for love, warmth and appreciation and with a proneness to react with depression to the frustration of these aspirations. Bibring described the narcissistic aspirations associated with the oral level as "the need to get affection, to be loved, to be taken care of, to get the 'supplies,' or by the opposite defensive need: to be independent, self-supporting."

While acknowledging the great frequency of oral fixations in the predisposition to depression and of the orally dependent type among those so predisposed, he appealed to clinical experience to substantiate his thesis that self-esteem may be decreased in other ways than by the frustration of the need for affection and love. He outlined how self-esteem can be lowered and depression brought about by the frustration of other narcissistic aspirations, e.g., of "the wish to be good, not to be resentful, hostile, defiant, but to be loving, not to be dirty, but to be clean, etc." which he associated not with the oral but with the anal phase. Depression over the lack of fulfillment of these aspirations will be colored by feelings of lack of control and weakness, i.e., by feelings of being too weak to control the libidinal and aggressive impulses or of guilt at this lack of control.

He described still another set of narcissistic aspirations which he believed were associated with the phallic phase. He characterized these as "the wish to be strong, superior, great, secure, not to be weak and insecure." The depression and the loss of self-esteem resulting from the frustration of these wishes will be colored by feelings of inadequacy and inferiority.

He believed that the frustration of any of these wishes will lead to a feeling of helplessness and a decrease of self-esteem. Since the infant of the oral phase is so realistically helpless, he considered it understandable that so many incidents predisposing to depression arise in this phase. He argued however that "any severe frustration of the little child's vital needs in and beyond the oral phase" will achieve the same result, except that the situations which will precipitate depressions in later life will have different characteristics.

Another major deviation of Bibring's was his concept of depression as an ego-phenomenon. It had been customary to think that depression was brought about by an inter-systemic conflict, i.e., by a conflict between the ego and the superego. Bibring however conceptualized depression as stemming from conflict or tension within the ego itself. Just as Freud (e.g.,1936) came to think of the ego as the site of anxiety so did Bibring also consider depression to be an affective state which is, like anxiety, a "state of the ego." He defined it as "the emotional expression (indication) of a state of helplessness and powerlessness of the ego, irrespective of what may have caused the breakdown of the mechanisms which established [the] self-esteem."

Rado in his earlier paper (1928) and Fenichel (1945) were the two chief defenders of the thesis that all depressive processes were carried out according to the same mechanism. This mechanism can be described as the loss of self-esteem and the resulting struggle to win back narcissistic supplies. Fenichel stated that "the whole depressive process appears as an attempt at reparation, intended to restore the self-esteem that has been damaged." This formula was broad enough to cover both neurotic and psychotic types of depression. The distinction between the two lay in the observation that the object from which the neurotic was trying to wrest narcissistic supplies was still an external object, one in the outer world. In the case of the melancholic however the "pathognomonic introjection" had taken place. It will be noted that it was the two components of loss of self-esteem and propitiation of the love object which characterized the alleged similarity of all depressions. It was merely the extent of the turning away from reality that determined their difference.

Bibring, as was indicated above, also saw all depressions as having a common basic structure. This common "core of normal, neurotic and probably also psychotic depression" is the loss of self-esteem, the ego's painful awareness of its helplessness to achieve its aspirations. But unlike Rado and Fenichel he did not see all depressions as attempts at reparation. Instead, he saw these reparative attempts as reactions to the depression, i.e., to the loss of self-esteem.

He assumed that the various clinical depressive syndromes represent "complications" of the basic type of depression. He acknowledged that depression is frequently accompanied by self-accusations and self-reproaches but he disagreed with the deduction from this that all depressive reactions are therefore a redirection of object-directed aggression against the self. He did not question the validity of the classical theories of the role which aggression or oral strivings play in certain types of depression. But he did challenge the universality of these phenomena.

He felt that his formulation about the basic mechanism in depression was broad enough to include grief and the exhaustion type of depression. In the former he believed that the depression derives from the fact that the ego is confronted with an inescapable situation, one in which it does not have the power to undo. And in the latter also he argued that the ego is faced with a situation of powerlessness which it is unable to solve.

In summary, Bibring reduced the multiplicity of depressive conditions to what he considered their lowest common denominator, a loss of self-esteem, designating all other manifestations of depression as secondary "complicating" phenomena. He thus succeeded in indicating that all depressive reactions have something in common without at the same time denying that depressed states exhibit a complexity and multiplicity of forms.

He gave explicit recognition to the several ways in which depressives experience their unhappiness, and with this insight he found himself forced to deny the universality of oral fixations in depressed conditions.

His conceptualization of depression as an ego phenomenon or experience leads directly to one of the most complex and least understood problems in psychoanalytic theory. It would take one much too far afield to discuss this subject adequately in a review such as this, and as a matter of fact the present development of the theory of affects is still too incomplete to throw much light on this subject at this time. The reader however might be referred to papers by Benedek (1953), Jacobson (1953a) and Rapaport (1953), three contributors to this highly difficult subject.

3. JACOBSON (1)

With the consideration of Edith Jacobson's (1943, 1946, 1953, 1954, 1954a, 1954b, 1957) contributions to the subject of depression a new level of discourse is reached, a level both complex and subtle in presentation and content and yet precise and sharp in conceptualization. She constructs a comprehensive and elaborate formulation which is offered as a key to the understanding of states of mind as seemingly diverse as normal self-regard, depressive moods and psychotic states. Her papers are too numerous and lengthy to permit of any but the briefest and sketchiest of outlines. Her theoretical model is a very closely-knit and interlocking construction. It is based on a painstaking exposition of the development of the self, ego identifications, the ego-ideal and the superego. In order to make her theory of depression comprehensible it will be necessary to review this development as she visualizes it. It is however not entirely novel. It is solidly based on classical analytic theories, many of them previously outlined in the pages of this review. But her model is no mere recapitulation of previous conceptions of psychological development. She tries particularly to eradicate terminological imprecisions and to give body and detail to previously more sketchy expositions of ego identifications, ego-ideal formation and other concepts.

Although the purpose here is to review her theories only in so far as they throw light on the subject of depression, they nevertheless provide the opportunity to view the depressive states in useful perspective against the background of normal develpment. Her theory concerns itself with the pathology of self-esteem but it is first necessary to study the development and the anatomy of this self-esteem as she presents it.

She makes use of and incorporates earlier ideas about depression in a manner that illustrates the organic growth of these theories, so related are her concepts to what had been thought before and so natural a development are they from the earlier formulations. Although she disagrees with Bibring on several crucial points, her observations have convinced her too of the great number of sources from which depressed states may arise. She too is impressed, as was hinted above, with the central importance of the loss of self-esteem in depression. And she too acknowledges a difference between neurotic and psychotic depressions.

She examines this whole subject using the concepts, greatly elaborated, of the new psychoanalytic ego psychology about which a few words are in order at this point. In his remarks on the psychoanalytic theory of the ego, Hartmann (1950) takes care to distinguish more carefully than had been done previously between the meanings of the words "ego" and "self." The former is an abstraction used to refer to one particular psychic system in contradistinction to the other personality substructures, the id and the superego. The word "self" refers to one's own person as distinguished from other persons or things, or, to use the rather clumsy terminology, from other person- or thing-objects. Hartmann also makes use of the term "self-representation" which Jacobson has also extensively adopted. This term refers to the "endopsychic representations of our bodily and mental self in the system ego," the self-image. An analogous term is "object-representation." These self- and object-representations are cathected by libidinous or aggressive energy, according to this conceptual model. If, for example, the self-representation is highly cathected with libidinous energy, one's self-esteem is said to be high, since self-esteem is in large measure considered to be a reflection of the type of cathexis, whether libidinous or aggressive, of the self-image.

Our self-image is said to derive essentially from two sources: first, from the direct perception and awareness of our inner feelings, experiences, sensations and thoughts, and secondly, from a more detached and introspective perception of our bodies, thoughts and emotions as objects. The latter is of course much more "intellectual" than directly felt and is proportionately secondary in importance in our conception of ourself which tends to fluctuate more in accordance with our emotional experience.

According to Jacobson (1954b) our self-image is at first not a firm unit. It is derived from sensations which are scarcely distinguished in infancy from perceptions of the gratifying part-object (the breast) and it is therefore at first fused and confused with object-images. Rather than being an enduring concept it is made up of an incessantly changing series of self-images derived from the continual fluctuations of the primitive mental state.

She postulates that some of the most fundamental goals of development are the integration, organization and unification of these images into a firm and consistent self-image, the establishment of stable and enduring boundaries between the self- and object-representations and the optimal cathexis of these representations with libidinous energy. In other words these goals include the firm establishment of one's own identity, the clear differentiation of one's self from others, the development and maintenance of an optimal level of self-esteem and the capacity to form satisfactory object-relationships.

These goals can best be reached in an atmosphere of parental care and affection in which tolerable frustrations are experienced in manageable doses. There are dangers from two directions. Over-gratification with undue prolongation of the mother-child unit will delay the establishment of firm boundaries between self- and object-images and will retard the development of independence and the formation of a realistic view of the outer world. Excessive frustrations, beyond the capacity of the developing ego to master them, will result in an immoderately aggressive cathexis of object- and self-images with unsatisfying interpersonal attitudes and feelings of inferiority and self-disparagement.

Jacobson (1954b) outlines in considerable detail her theory of the development of ego identifications. Although it is not in every respect original, (which indeed it is not claimed to be) it is nevertheless characterized by a noteworthy thoroughness of conceptualization. She considers that ego identifications develop through essentially three stages: 1. the fusion of the child's self-image with the image of his mother; 2. the child's imitation of his love objects; 3. his real modification of himself to become like his parents.

She considers participation in the mother-child unit to be the earliest stage in infancy. She believes that the child can discriminate between himself and his mother only after the function of perception develops. She considers that it is frustration particularly that makes the infant aware of the distinction between himself and the object. Frustration, deprivation and separation from the mother cause the infant to become aware of himself as a separate entity from his mother. Theoretically these also lead to wishful fantasies of reunion. When the infant nurses or is close to his mother these wishful fantasies are gratified and the images of the self and the mother are presumed to merge again. "Thus the hungry infant's longing for oral gratification is the origin of the first, primitive type of identification, an identification achieved by refusion of self- and object-images and founded on wishful fantasies of oral incorporation of the love object. This refusion of self- and object-images will be accompanied by a temporary weakening of the perceptive functions and hence by a return from the level of beginning ego formation to an earlier, less differentiated state." *

The next phase in the development of ego identifications is said to consist of the child's increasing attempts to imitate his love objects. Identification is now sought by imitation. The child begins early to notice, respond to and emulate the gestures, actions and emotions of the mother. His maturing speech and motor facility, his ability to talk and move around, in short his developing ego activities are all used in the service of being "like" his mother. There are magic illusory components to this type of imitation. They "indicate how much the child wants to maintain the mother as a part of himself and to adhere to the primitive aims of identification: the merging of maternal and self-images without distinction of and regard for the external and his own, inner reality."

It is during this period that the infant is considered to be learning to tolerate his ambivalence. This learning process is characterized by "constant cathectic shifts and changes" in which libido and aggression are continuously turned from the self to the love object and back again, or from one object to another. Frequent fusions and separations of the self- and object-images occur in this phase. Sometimes one image is cathected only with libido, while all the aggression is directed to another one. This will go on until ambivalence can be tolerated and distinct images can be cathected with mixtures of both love and hate. During this period of marked cath-

---

*Therese Benedek (1956) describes the nursing process in a similar way: "The mother becomes with each nursing and feeding, part of the self again."

ectic changes "the child will display submissive clinging attitudes or behavior alternating with temporary grandiose ideas showing his 'magic participation' in the parents' omnipotence. There will be erratic vacillations between attitudes of passive, helpless dependency on the omnipotent mother and active, aggressive strivings for self-sufficient independence or for a powerful control over the love objects."

It is worth repeating that it is the child's still not fully developed ability to distinguish between internal and external reality, his poor reality testing in other words, that is said to be so important in maintaining the haziness and weakness of the endopsychic boundaries between the self- and object-images. And it is this haziness that is thought to facilitate the exaggerated cathectic shifts between them. It is this same developmental immaturity that is believed to allow the child to distort the images of his love objects until they conform to his own wishful fantasies, or to project onto them those undesirable features of himself that he wishes to disown, or to aggrandize his own self-image with their admired attributes. All this is presumed to derive from the lack of adequate distinction between the child's images of himself and his parents and from his incomplete ability to discriminate between his images of objects and the objects themselves. The world of the pre-oedipal child is a magical world which is characterized by fantasies that he is part of his parents or that he becomes identified with them by imitating them or pretending to be them. It is this period of the child's life that is most marked by belief in the omnipotence of thought and in the magic of words.

This pre-oedipal magic world is not necessarily entirely relinquished. Remnants of it survive in the attitudes and fantasies of adults and it is to this stage that the psychotic ego is thought to regress. Whether or not the metapsychological explanations and theoretical reconstructions of this developmental stage are accepted, the magical world itself, the omnipotent fantasies and the hazy boundaries between the concepts of the self and of objects have all been extensively observed and documented in the voluminous literature on child psychology and clinical psychiatry. Werner (1940) in particular is worth mentioning for his valuable comparative study of the thinking of the child, the primitive and the psychotic.

In the later stages of ego identification the child does not strive for complete unity with his parents, nor are his efforts necessarily directed towards the imitation of his love objects. Instead, he utilizes a more mature form of identification. His efforts are now directed towards becoming *like* his parents by a real modification of the self and the self-image as he takes over many of their attitudes and interests and ways of behaving. Before he can do this of course there must be a more or less firm boundary between his self- and object-representations. And he must have reached a point where he is able to have a distinct conception of his parents' mental and bodily characteristics. Jacobson also discusses the vicissitudes of the sexual identifications with the oedipal rival in this eventful period.

Not only are ego identifications now established but the parental standards, prohibitions and demands are also gradually internalized and comprise the basis of superego identifications and self-critical superego functions. The precursors of the superego system in the pre-oedipal stage are said to be the first reaction formations. Parental attitudes cause revisions in the attitude of the child towards himself and the world of objects. If successful, these reaction formations permeate all mental areas. "Thus the reaction formations acquired during bowel training will show, first, in ideas that feces are dirty and belong in the toilet and children who soil are bad; second, in feelings of disgust at the bowels, of shame at loss of bowel control, of pride in achieving cleanliness and of pleasure in clean, neat, and beautiful things; and third, in active efforts to move the bowels punctually on the toilet, to keep clean and to accept the meaning of time, the routine of life and schedules in general. Additionally and secondarily, aesthetic interests and the urge for artistic creation may develop, indicative of a beginning sublimation of anal drives." It should be mentioned that Jacobson recognizes other roots than bowel training in the development of the above mentioned reaction formations.

One type of reaction that plays an important role during this period of bowel training is considered by Jacobson to have wider significance also. This is the reaction of devaluation or depreciation. As the child suffers frustrating and disappointing experiences at the hands of his love objects he entertains, at first perhaps fleeting, but later more persistent conscious and unconscious derogatory and hostile feelings, thoughts and impulses toward them. If too pronounced or too early, they endanger the establishment of his self-esteem, which is so dependent on his respect and affection for his love objects. But this type of disillusionment in his parents, if not too extreme, plays a beneficial role in the development of his sense of reality and in the giving up by the child of his magical fantasies about his parents and himself.

However, besides devaluation, there is another tendency at work during this developmental period, one which aids the child in his struggle with these feelings of hostility. This is the tendency to idealize his love objects. The remnants of the magic belief in their omnipotence and value become split off from the more realistic appraisal of their worth and powers and become moulded into the ego ideal.

It is postulated that in the pre-oedipal child there are close connections between the self- and object-images and that the devaluation of the parent has a tendency to increase self-devaluation, just as has the painfully dawning awareness of the lack of one's personal omnipotence. In a similar way, and counteracting all this, the self-image shares in this process of idealization and thus the "narcissistic wounds" are helped to heal. "Forever close to the id and yet indispensable for the ego, the ego ideal is eventually molded from . . . idealized object- and self-images and set up as part of the superego system, as a pilot and guide for the ego."

The ego ideal is composed of more than the idealized parents however. The establishment of the ego ideal is saved from becoming merely a survival of magic fantasies and images by the advancing maturation of the ego functions of discrimination and judgment. These allow the distinction to be maintained between the "real" parents and the idealized images and they permit this idealization to be extended to "abstract values in general, to ideas, ideals and ideal pursuits." Compromises are made between irrational yearnings and rational necessities. The magical, idealized self- and object-images survive in part of the ego as abstract models of what we would like to become even though these goals may never be achieved. This longing to become like the ego-ideal stimulates ego development so that in counteracting self-devaluation it is next in importance to parental love "which is of course the best guarantee for a sound development of object-relations and self-esteem."

Jacobson considers that self-esteem, the emotional expression of self-evaluation, represents the degree of discrepancy or harmony between the self-representations and the wished-for concept of the self. This way of looking at self-esteem bears a resemblance to that of Bibring (1953) who speaks of self-esteem as "the tension between . . . . highly charged narcissistic aspirations on the one hand, and the ego's acute awareness of its (real and imaginary) helplessness and incapacity to live up to them on the other hand."

Jacobson's description, however, of the factors involved in self-esteem seems much more encompassing and comprehensive. She considers the variables involved to be as follows:

1. *The superego.* By virtue of the experience of guilt which is the expression of superego fear, the superego exercises an enormous influence over our feelings, thoughts and actions. Any discrepancy between these and the ego ideal brings about an increased aggressive cathexis of the self-representations since the superego is considered to be endowed with both libidinal and aggressive energy.

2. *The self-critical ego functions.* With the maturation of the ego and the increasing ability to discriminate between the reasonable and the unreasonable, our concepts of value and our actions are considerably modified. The more mature the self-critical ego functions are, the more tempered and realistic will be our idealism and expectations and goals. The less unattainable our ideal, the less vulnerable is our self-esteem.

3. *The ego ideal.* The more within reach this is, the more prone it is to stimulate ego activity to live up to it and thus to enhance self-esteem. But, according to Annie Reich (1953) who has paid particular attention to the study of the ego ideal, "An over-grandiose ego ideal—combined as it not infrequently is, with inadequate talents and insufficient ego strength—leads to intolerable inner conflicts and feelings of insufficiency."

4. *The ego functions.* It is clear that the degree of success in measuring up to the demands of the ego ideal has a considerable influence on the level of self-esteem.

5. *The self-representations.* Pathological development of the self-representations, for any reason, will of course have an important effect on the self-esteem.

Jacobson indicates the broad base of her concept of self-esteem by her comment: "Increase or decrease of libidinous or aggressive discharge, inhibition or stimulation of ego functions, libidinous impoverishment or enrichment of the self caused by external or internal factors, from somatic, psychosomatic, or psychological sources, may induce or enhance the libidinous or aggressive cathexis of the self-representations and lead to fluctuations of self-esteem." In other words, success or failure, good or bad health, affection and love or neglect and dislike from the earliest or the most current love objects all have an effect on the libidinous or aggressive cathexis of the self-image, i.e., on the self-esteem.

It is worth while considering one of these determinants of self-esteem, the ego ideal, in a little more detail. As will be remembered, idealization is considered to be a very important process which serves to protect the child against the feelings of depreciation that he entertains towards his parents and towards himself. Annie Reich (1953) considers that the ego ideal "is based upon the desire to cling in some form or another to a denial of the ego's as well as the parent's limitations and to regain infantile omnipotence by identifying with the idealized parent."

In an interesting paper (1954) she studies a few cases in which the ego ideals were unattainable either because they were too grandiose and too omnipotent or else because the ability to translate these goals into goal-directed activity was lacking. In these patients she describes fluctuations in self-esteem which occurred because on the one hand there was an awareness of the failure to reach the goal and on the other hand there was an intermittent blurring of reality testing sufficient to allow the patient to feel that he had actually attained his goal.

In another study of pathological identifications, Rochlin (1953) also describes a group of patients with fluctuations of mood. These fluctuations were of sufficient magnitude for him to refer to the condition as "the disorder of depression and elation." His cases, although he does not describe them as doing so, confirm several aspects of Bibring's and Jacobson's theories. For one thing the patients he describes do not complain of being unloved or of being guilty, but of being weak and inadequate. This is a result of what Rochlin describes as conflicts on the phallic level of development, although elements of previous phases are also incorporated into their psychopathology. In each of his four cases he shows that the self-devaluation sprang from an identification with a devalued mother and a wish to be like the idealized father who is conceived in very phallic terms. His cases illustrate Jacobson's formulation of the determinants of self-esteem although Rochlin makes no reference to her theory nor does he use her terminology. There is present in his patients a grandiose and unattainable ego ideal, a severely critical superego, an impairment of the self-critical functions and an inability by ego functions or ego activity alone to attain to the ego ideal, all resulting in an immoderately aggressive cathexis of the self-image, in other words, in loss of self-esteem and depression. Like Annie Reich's cases, his patients had episodes when their ability to differentiate their ideal from themselves became impaired and in which they became elated because of the magical fusion of their ego ideals with their self-representations.

4. JACOBSON (2)

Having digressed in order to consider in more detail one of the determinants of self-esteem, namely the ego ideal, and the part that it plays in fluctuations of mood, let us now return to Jacobson's (1953, 1954) views on self-esteem and depression. As was indicated previously she considers these two states to be intimately related. She believes that loss of self-esteem, (or in other words, feelings of inferiority, weakness, impoverishment and helplessness) represents "the central psychological problem in depression." All the factors that can be included among the determinants of self-esteem then can also be considered as having important relevance for depression.

Jacobson distinguishes between neurotic and psychotic depressive reactions. She considers that the self-esteem is diminished in both but that psychotic patients sustain in addition "a severe regressive process in the whole personality organization." She agrees with Freud (1917) that psychotic depressions have somatic components which can not be explained on a psychological basis alone.

She feels that psychotics are predisposed to their severe regressions by a defective ego and superego development which remains fixated at an immature pre-oedipal level. This impaired development is considered to be a result both of their inherited constitutions and of their early infantile emotional deprivations and frustrations. It will be remembered that Jacobson postulates that solid ego and superego identifications can only develop in an atmosphere of parental love and care. In such an atmosphere, the self- and object-images become sharply separated and the magical, idealized, primitive qualities of the self and the love objects are depersonified and retained in an ego ideal distinct and separate from these self- and object-images. The parental commands and standards are also depersonified and integrated into a superego system.

Severe disappointments in the first years of life bring about a premature devaluation of the love objects. This interferes with the normal establishment of self-esteem by virtue of the identification with the love object that exists at this stage. In other words, the self-image shares in the aggressive cathexis of the object-representations because of their incomplete separation and their tendency to fuse and coalesce. If the parent is prematurely devaluated, the child "must get involved in the collapse of the magic world , . . . (and he) may swing from an optimistic to a pessimistic illusion which again distorts reality." Jacobson believes that this premature and excessive disappointment in the parents with the accompanying devaluation of them—and the self—occurs in the early life of depressive patients and helps to explain the fixation of their ego and superego identifications at pre-oedipal levels.

The prepsychotic personality has many of the characteristics of this pre-oedipal magic stage of personality development. "The self- and object-representations and the ego ideal will not be sharply separated; they will retain attributes of early infantile object- and self-images . . . The superego will not be a firmly integrated system. It will be personified, unstable in its functions, and will tend either to assume excessive control of the ego or to disintegrate, dissolve, and merge with object- and self-representations. It will be easily reprojected on the outside world." The superego, object- and self-representations will be prone, in times of stress, to lose their distinctness and boundaries, such as they are. They will tend to fuse together regressively until they are indistinguishable from one another or else to split into even more primitive early images. The prepsychotic person will tend to handle his conflicts with methods characteristic of the pre-oedipal phase such as massive withdrawals and shifts of aggressive and libidinal cathexis from object to self or from object to object.

Jacobson emphasizes the unusual degree of dependency which these cyclothymic patients display. Their objects need not necessarily be persons since they are just as capable of establishing intense emotional ties to causes or organizations of a political, scientific or religious nature. These persons or causes become ideal powerful love objects upon which they become very dependent for love or moral supoprt. As was mentioned previously, the cyclothymic patient's object-representations are insufficiently separated from the parental component of the ego ideal and are therefore correspondingly and unrealistically idealized. It is this over-evaluation which permits these patients who feel themselves to be so helpless and weak to become so dependent on their love-objects for strength and support.

This type of exaggerated dependency is closely linked to what Jacobson regards as a "specific ego weakness" in these patients, namely their extreme intolerance to hurt, frustration or disappointment. Failings in the love object or in the self are both prone to precipitate depressive states. In either case the patient tends to feel hurt and disappointed and to put blame on the love object.

And since the object is so excessively idealized it is inevitable that it will eventually fail to live up to the patient's expectations. This intolerance to hurt and disappointment represents an important and particularly characteristic vulnerability in this type of person. One defense against this tendency to be disappointed in the love object is the mechanism of denial, the denial of weakness or inadequacy in the love object. And this same mechanism serves in another way to keep the patient in a dependent position since it conceals from him his own intrinsic worth and promotes his tendency to see himself as a weak and helpless person.

This presentation of Jacobson's concept of depression has necessitated the consideration of several different aspects of this rather complex subject. It might be helpful at this point to pull these different theoretical strands together by glancing back briefly over the material that has been reviewed thus far. Her version of the way in which ego and superego identifications develop has been discussed. An outline has been given of her description of the maturation of the self- and object-representations. This, as will be remembered, involves a development through passive and active pre-oedipal magical phases into the period of stable, enduring self- and object-images. These images, as Jacobson thinks of them, are sharply separated from one another and from the ego ideal and superego systems which represent the de-personified and abstract remnants of the early omnipotent and magic images of the parents and the self. The relationship of these metapsychological concepts to her understanding of the development and maintenance of self-esteem has been described. Attention has also been drawn to Jacobson's observations on the constitutional and developmental predisposition to psychotic depression, on the specific vulnerability of the prepsychotic manic-depressive to feelings of hurt and disappointment and on the characteristic defense of denial which this type of patient employs to master his narcissistic injuries.

To return to the cyclothymic patient's reaction to loss and disappointment, Jacobson observes that the denial mechanism may be so augmented that the patient may lose touch with reality and go into a manic state. Jacobson believes that this manic phase represents "a state of lasting participation of the self in the imagined omnipotence of the love-object," a view of elation which corresponds to the conceptions of Annie Reich (1953, 1954) and Rochlin (1953).

If on the other hand the denial mechanism breaks down and this phase does not occur the patient may try to undo his narcissistic injury by drastic cathectic changes. He will shift all the aggressive cathexis to the object-image while transferring the whole libidinous cathexis to the self-image, i.e., he will assert himself by renouncing and derogating the love-object. This self-inflation, in contrast to that described in the previous paragraph, is associated with a devaluation of the love-object rather than with a participation in its omnipotence. This is an untenable position for the manic-depressive. He "cannot bear a self-assertion through derogation of his love-object. . . . . He is so afraid of a lasting self-inflation at the expense of the love-object, because it might lead to a complete libidinous withdrawal and a letting loose of all his severe hostility on this one object."

He will therefore become hyperaware of any defects in himself or in his achievements and there will be a rapid reversal of the previous situation with a reflux of aggression from the object- to the self-image. All this of course is reflected in marked vacillations of mood. However, it may happen that he is no longer fully able to recathect the object. All that is left for him in that case is an aggressive devaluation of both himself and the love-object. This phase of depression Jacobson refers to as "the primary depressive disturbance" and it consists of a pessimistic, disillusioned, uninterested attitude to life and to the self which makes everything seem empty, worthless and without pleasure.

Jacobson has observed that some patients will now make use of what she refers to as secondary attempts at defense and restitution. The patient, in order to replenish his depleted libidinal resources may turn for narcissistic supplies to some object other than his former love-object. He will attach to him his ideal object-images and will hope to function through the magic love that he expects to obtain from this person. He will desperately gather all of his available libido and pour it on this individual in an attitude of clinging submission. He will, in effect, "try to blackmail him into a continuous show of omnipotent love, value, and power." If he happens to be a patient in treatment he may, at this point, direct his massive demands towards the therapist.

If this attempt does not succeed, the depressive may then go one step further. In his desperate need he may give up his hope for an infinitely loving object and may attempt to settle for a love object that is at least strong and powerful. "The patient may now attempt to hold on at least to the reanimated image of an omnipotent, not loving, but primitive sadistic object. This will manifest itself in the patient's increasing masochistic provocations of the analyst's anger, to a show of aggression, which may bring temporary relief but will actually promote the pathological process."

If this maneuver also fails, the patient may then resort to his last restitutive attempt, to his last line of defense, the final retreat from the object world. In her description of this mechanism Jacobson follows closely upon Rado's (1928) conception of the last weapon to win back love and regain self-esteem, except that she rephrases it in the more detailed and precise language that is characteristic of her formulations. It will be remembered that Freud (1917) recognized the self-accusations of the melancholic to be essentially accusations against the abandoned love-object, now identified with the self. Rado however felt that the self-condemnation of the depressive also represented an act of contrition to win back the love of the archetypical love-object, the superego who has now replaced the abandoned love-object. As Rado put it: "The melancholic has transferred the scene of his struggle for the love of his object to a different stage. He has withdrawn in narcissistic fashion to the inner world of his own mind and now, instead of procuring the pardon and love of his object, he tries to secure those of his superego."

He felt that in the appeasement of the superego, the ego tries to win back the love not only of the original love object but also of the latest love object, the good aspects of which have been introjected into the superego, the internalized fount and source of all goodness and love. Thus Rado conceived the abandoned love-object to have been split into two parts. Its "bad" aspect, "the bad object" has been introjected into the ego and punished while its "good" aspect, that aspect of it which was formerly loved, has been introjected into the superego and supplicated.

Jacobson restates much of this but with greater terminological precision. She emphasizes the continuity of this restitutive process with the earlier methods of maintaining self-esteem. It will be recalled that one of the secondary attempts at restitution involved the setting up of a powerful, primitive object-representation in the ego and the desperate effort to force the real object to conform to this picture. Jacobson (1953) postulates that in the melancholic psychotic phase "this reanimated, inflated image will now be dissolved as a representation in the system ego and will be absorbed by the superego, whereas the deflated worthless object-image merges with the self-representations."

In her theory it is not the object which is split up but instead the object-image. The deflated worthless object-image merges not with the ego, as was previously thought, but with the self-representations.

The powerful but primitive object-image merges with the superego. These fusions are facilitated, in Jacobson's view, by the inadequate initial separation of the self- and object-images from one another and from the superego. In other words, Jacobson considers the melancholic psychotic process to consist of a regressive dissolution of the identifications which had been precariously built up in the prepsychotic manic-depressive, a dissolution which results in fusions of bad or good love-object images with the self-image and with the superego and which leads to a very pathological conflict between the self and the superego.

Freud (1917) had referred to the melancholic process as one of "narcissistic identification." Jacobson, as we see, prefers to think of what happens not as an identification of ego with the object but as a partial or total fusion of the self- and object-images in the system ego. In this type of identification the ego does not assume the characteristics of the love object. Instead, the self is experienced or treated as though it actually were the love object. In her own terminology it would perhaps be more proper to speak merely of an introjection rather than an identification since no actual transformation of the ego, characteristic of identification, takes place. What happens rather is that the self-representations take on the characteristics of the object-images by a process of fusion.

Jacobson, believing that this regressive process represents but a continuation of previous attempts at restitution and defense, points out that in the manic-depressive's retreat from the object world and in his internalization of the conflict, he is still trying to reconstitute a powerful love object but now in the superego rather than in the external world. She conceives of the self in this intra-psychic continuation of the struggle with the love object as being as helpless and powerless as a small child who is dependent upon and being punished by a cruel, primitive parent. She also draws attention to the fact that this inner feeling of helplessness and inadequacy is augmented by the actual inhibition of ego functions that the melancholic experiences.

To review Jacobson's contribution to the theory of depression, what she has done is in essence, as follows: She has asserted that the loss of self-esteem is the central psychological problem in depression and has examined the determinants of this self-esteem. She has moreover described the mechanisms which the prepsychotic manic-depressive uses to maintain his precarious self-esteem and she has outlined some of the restitutive maneuvers he employs to regain it once it is lost. It is in this theoretical scheme that she has fitted in the manic-depressive's last restitutive maneuver, the final withdrawal from reality with its characteristic introjection of the love object, a mechanism which previous authors had studied so intensively and sometimes so exclusively. She has furthermore suggested that the manic-depressive's ability to resort to this psychotic restitutive maneuver is dependent not simply on early traumata but more specifically on an incomplete and pathological development of ego and supergo identifications.

She believes that it is insufficient to say that there is a libidinal regression to the oral phase. Moreover, to say simply that there is also an ego regression in psychotic depression is for her also insufficiently informative and precise. It is therefore her particular contribution to have ventured beyond this formula and to have attempted to clarify the nature of this ego regression. Her theory that what happens is, in the first place an insufficient maturation and separation of self- and object-images and ego ideal and superego systems, and in the second place, a regressive dissolution of these identifications, represents a provocative attempt to offer a sophisticated, although perhaps too speculative conception of an important depressive mechanism.

5. COHEN

The report from Chestnut Lodge entitled *An Intensive Study of Twelve Cases of Manic-Depressive Psychosis* is worthy of review for the very pertinent observations and conclusions it contains. Mabel Blake Cohen and a group of co-workers (1954) have written what is essentially an empirical study of a small group of manic-depressive patients. This study is very far removed, on the face of it, from the type of metapsychological speculation so characteristic of Jacobson's work. The language employed in this paper is basically Sullivanian and even words like "superego" are assiduously avoided. Yet the concepts are visibly related to those of Rado, Jacobson, Melanie Klein and others. The similarity of many of this group's observations to those of Jacobson will be especially apparent in a later chapter when their respective views on the treatment of manic-depressive psychosis will be considered. In view of the terminological differences it is interesting to note that Cohen and her colleagues consider that the approach of Melanie Klein is closest to their own thinking.

The authors' intention in this study was to discover those experiences with significant people which made it necessary for the future manic-depressive to develop his characteristic patterns of interaction. They stress not single traumatic events but "the interpersonal environment from birth on", which, interacting with the constitutional endowment, produces the manic-depressive.

The authors report certain similarities in the family backgrounds of their patients. Each family was in some way "different" from others in the community either because it belonged to a minority group or because it was in worse (or in one case much superior) economic circumstances or because one parent was alcoholic or psychotic. The families were keenly aware of this difference and reacted to it by striving to conform to the neighbors' standards or by trying to augment their prestige by accomplishments of one kind or another. The children were used in this struggle for prestige and were expected to conform to the strict and conventional code of good behavior attributed to "them," the envied neighbors. The parents' approval of the children was contingent on what they accomplished whether in the form of grades, medals or teachers' praise. The child destined to be a manic-depressive was often selected as the family's standard-bearer in this battle for prestige because of his superior gifts or beauty or because of his position in the family.

The mother was prone to depreciate her husband and was usually ambitious and aggressive and the stronger and more determined and stable parent. The fathers of these manic-depressive patients were usually unsuccessful, weak men who complained of their wives' contempt and coldness. Paradoxically the patients loved their fathers much more warmly than their mothers and tended to defend and justify them. Thus the unreliable contemptible parent was also the loved one whereas the reliable, strong parent was the disliked one.

This study is valuable in that it is the only one that has specifically examined the family backgrounds of manic-depressive patients. The authors however are cautious about generalizing too widely from their relatively small group. They feel that a statistical study of the problem is needed to confirm or refute their findings. One must agree that this would be desirable. One's own clinical experience and a review of the case histories in the literature would tend to arouse doubts as to the universality of just this particular type of family background in the lives of all manic-depressive patients.

Melanie Klein (1948) had earlier suggested that every child in the course of normal develpment has to come to terms with his increasing awareness that his mother could some times be "good" and satisfying and at other times "bad" and denying. She argued that this awareness that his "good object" could at any time become "bad" is so troublesome to the child and so productive of depressive anxieties that he has to resort to various defensive techniques to hide this from himself until such time as he has firmly internalized his good object and has acquired the necessary confidence that his good object will return even if it does leave him temporarily or becomes for a time denying or frustrating.

One of the most important of these techniques is the regressive splitting of the mother into a "good mother"—always bountiful and satisfying—and a "bad mother" who is rejecting and unsatisfying and who can be hated unreservedly. That the satisfying and the rejecting aspects of the mother are really different facets of the same person are thus denied. The mother at any given time is by the use of this technique either all black or all white and the child is defended against the anxieties of having to view her as a complex multi-faceted individual.

Mabel Blake Cohen and her group believe that this denial of the complexity of people, this insistence on seeing them as either all black or all white persists in the adult manic-depressive and is a distinguishing characteristic of his interpersonal relationships. They feel that the persistence of this defense can be attributed to the greater than average difficulty that these patients as children had in integrating the different aspects of their mothers into a unified picture.

The research group noted that the mothers of these patients found their children more acceptable when they were infants and presumably more dependent than when they began to assert themselves with increasing rebelliousness and independence. The children found their hitherto tender, loving mothers abruptly changing into harsh, punitive figures at about the end of their first year. It appeared to the writers that these attitudes were more strikingly different from one another than in the lives of other more fortunate children and were correspondingly more difficult to integrate into one picture of a whole human being, sometimes affectionate and sometimes punitive, sometimes "good" and sometimes "bad." The patients as children learned to think of their parents as tyrannical punitive figures from whom good things could be expected only if they were not displeased by unconventional or unconforming behavior. The parents were powerful entities who had to be continually placated by good behavior.

These workers found that their patients, as children, felt keenly the responsibility of increasing the prestige of the family by personal accomplishments. This role tended to give them a considerably different picture of the significant members of the family from the ones their siblings had. These patients were extremely lonely people, often unconsciously so, despite the frequently clannish nature of the family. Their strangely pre-eminent positions in their families made them unconsciously afraid of the envy of their siblings and many of them developed a defensive pattern of underselling themselves in order to hide the full extent of their superiority. Another device used by these patients who were so sensitive to envy and competition was to be exceptionally helpful to their brothers and sisters and later on to other people. The fee they unconsciously demanded from their siblings and the successors of these siblings was complete acceptance and preference by them.

These cyclothymic patients, during their healthy periods, are described as being superficially well adjusted, despite perhaps some mild mood disturbances, conventional, hard working, conscientious individuals who have a considerable degree of social facility and often numerous but shallow relationships with people. They are however characteristically involved in one or a few relationships of extreme dependency. They are usually unconscious of this dependency even though their inner feeling may be one of emptiness and need. Demands are made for approval, love and service not necessarily in return for having met the reciprocal needs of their love-objects but because of what they consider to be their own sacrifices. These sacrifices seem to consist of the underselling of the self which appears to be unconsciously designed to avert the love-object's envy and to indicate their own need.

The authors stress the manic-depressive patient's incapacity for emotional give and take, and his insensitivity to interpersonal phenomena to the point where he is not even aware of the extent to which he may be irritating or annoying to the person from whom he has been trying to extort narcissistic supplies. He does not see other people as human beings who have their own individual reactions, responses and idiosyncracies. Instead he tends to see them as stereotypes. His interpersonal activities seem to consist of maneuvers designed to ensure the other's goodness and approval.

Cohen and her co-workers, like Bibring (1953) but unlike Melanie Klein (1934, 1940) and Jacobson (1953) feel that the manic-depressive's hostility has been considerably overstressed as a dynamic factor in his illness. They see hostile feelings in this condition as a secondary formation arising from the frustration of the patient's needs. Moreover, much of the hostility that has been attributed to the manic-depressive is considered by them to be the result of the annoyance he arouses in others by his demanding behavior, rather than a reflection of a primary wish to harm others.

The group's conception of the psychotic attack conforms in most of its essentials to formulations with which we are already familiar. It can be either a loss or a success that precipitates the attack because the important thing is that the event, whatever it is, is appraised by the patient as removing him from a position of relatively stable dependency. The patient then resorts to depressive techniques. He whines and complains and tries to elicit the gratifications he requires. These efforts fail because of their offensiveness but the attempt is renewed with redoubled energy. This continues until "he loses hope and enters into the psychotic state when the pattern of emptiness and need is repeated over and over again in the absence of any specific object . . . . The appeal may be mute, acted out by his despair, sleeplessness and inability to eat, or it may be highly vociferous and addressed verbally to all who come in contact with him, in the form of statements about his bowels being blocked up, his insides being empty, his family having been bankrupted or killed, and so on."

These authors feel that the manic-depressive does not suffer genuine guilt. They believe that he does not experience genuine feelings of regret and that he does not make any effort to modify his behavior. He sees the love-object as an authority figure who has certain expectations of him and who has to be placated. Guilt for such a patient is merely a means to an end. He makes no attempt to change the nature of his relationships. He merely depends on "the magic of uttering guilty cries to placate authority." Thus guilt and self-reproach are viewed by these writers as exploitative techniques and not as the result of a regressive identification with or introjection of the abandoned love-object.

To sum up, Mabel Blake Cohen and her colleagues have reported an empirical study of a small group of manic-depressives in the course of whose treatment they were able to delineate a typical family situation, a typical kind of parent-child relationship, a typical role performed for their families by these patients and, finally, a typical kind of personality structure with its characteristic pattern of interpersonal relationships. Although most of these factors have not previously been formally described as determinants of the manic-depressive personality, the cyclothymic personality structure as outlined by these writers has been, in most of its essentials, confirmed numerous times in the literature both in its descriptive (e.g. Titley, 1938; Palmer and Sherman, 1938) and in its dynamic aspects.

Although adopting many concepts about early development from previous writers, concepts which inevitably involve a certain amount of theorizing, Cohen *et al.* manifest a disinclination to engage in speculation. They prefer to concern themselves with the "interpersonal" aspects of their patients' illnesses and as a result appear not to find very useful the standard formulations about the introjection of the bad object. They prefer to see the guilty self-accusations as coercive maneuvers to obtain gratification of their dependency needs, a point of view which Rado also emphasizes, particularly in his more recent work (1951). It is in the study of the transference and counter-transference aspects of the treatment of these patients that this group's work is most valuable and this will be discussed in a later chapter.

Chapter IV

1. INTRODUCTION

WE HAVE TRACED the psychoanalytic concept of depression, noting its theoretical vicissitudes from the earliest reflections on oral traits in depressed patients through to the extensive ramifications of Jacobson's comprehensive theory. The aim has consistently been to delineate the major contributions to this theory, to set them in their proper perspective and to indicate their genetic relationship to previous observations and conceptualizations. There have been many aspects of the theory of depression which have been referred to rather fragmentarily. In studying the details of any one writer's contribution, there is some danger of losing perspective with regard to the more general direction and shape of the body of theory. It is difficult to examine a subject both longitudinally and in cross-section at the same time. In this chapter, therefore, in order to think about depression from another vantage point, we will consider separately the various strands that have gone into the weaving of this theoretical structure. Dissecting out its various components and examining each one of them separately in the light of the subject matter already reviewed should aid in allowing one to understand more clearly this sometimes confusing body of theory. We will briefly recapitulate and re-examine such elements of the theory of depression as the concepts of predisposition, pre-psychotic character structure, unconscious fantasies, aggression, orality, etc. with the aim of throwing more light upon them than was possible in the chronological account of the development of this theory.

2. HEREDITY

With regard to predisposition, although writer after writer has attempted to explain the etiology and mechanisms of depression in psychological terms, there has been evident a lingering feeling of discomfort and an underlying but varying degree of awareness that there was more to the depressive reaction than could be explained by environmental and experiential factors. Kraepelin regarded depression in its various manifestations as essentially a constitutional disease process. Meyer pointed out the therapeutic uselessness of such a focus and determinedly turned towards an examination of the potentially treatable factors in the reaction. Freud did not exclude the possibility that some types of melancholia were constitutional but of course proclaimed his field of interest to be the psychologically understandable features of the condition. But even in types of melancholia which he considered essentially psychogenic, he felt that some symptoms like diurnal variation were basically somatic in nature. Abraham in his effort to understand the choice of neurosis postulated that there was in depressives an inherited constitutional increased oral eroticism, a heightened capacity of the mucosa of the mouth to experience pleasure with an accompanying increased need and a consequent greater possibility of frustration of this need. Gero broadened the meaning of the term "orality" to include all manifestations of the need for dependency, love and warmth with the implication that in depressives, a heightened constitutional need of this kind stood in greater danger of frustration. Melanie Klein with her particular interest in early aggressive phenomena, postulated a "constitutionally strengthened oral sadism" as a possible factor in "the most serious deficiencies of development and psychic illnesses." Thus, these writers assumed that there exists in some people a constitutionally determined greater than average need for what is varyingly expressed as gratification of the oral erogenous zone or oral supplies in the wider sense. These increased needs, it was postulated, may lead to greater frustrations with a consequent greater tendency for fixation at the oral phase.

Jacobson (1953) with her interest in the ego psychological aspects of depression considers the question of predisposition in a somewhat different light. She first of all clearly distinguishes neurotic from psychotic depression and feels that the latter "represents not only a mental but an unknown psychosomatic process" and expresses the belief that this hypothesis will serve as an incentive to collaborative research on the biological, physiological and psychological aspects of psychosis. She believes that psychotic patients are predisposed to total regressive processes by an arrested, defective ego and superego development, the result of their inherited constitution and their infantile history.

Those geneticists who are interested in psychiatric problems do not attempt to isolate the individual factors that are inherited and constitutional in manic-depressive psychosis. They have been more concerned with determining if it is true at all that hereditary factors play a part in the etiology of this psychiatric disorder. Kallman (1948), perhaps the foremost American psychiatric geneticist has stated his views as follows: "The implication is that some persons have the genetic capacity for reacting to precipitating stimuli with either a schizophrenic or a manic-depressive type of psychosis, while others have not. Whether or not a real psychosis will be developed by such a 'predisposed' person usually depends on an intricate interplay of constitutional and environmental factors . . . . The specific nature of the respective genes is indicated by the observation that no twin partner has as yet been found with a schizophrenic psychosis in one member and with a manic-depressive psychosis in the other, if a consistent system of classification is used."

There are other writers however, (e.g., Penrose, 1945), who, while agreeing that this psychosis is hereditary, question the genetic specificity of the manic-depressive heredity.

Kallman (1953) defends his position however by maintaining that the presence of "small contingents of schizophrenics found among the relatives of manic-depressive patients" in some of the European studies merely reflects the looseness of the criteria for the diagnosis of manic-depressive psychosis in these studies. In his work, he carefully restricts the diagnosis to those "cyclic cases which showed periodicity of acute, self-limited mood swings before the fifth decade of life and no progressive or residual personality disintegration before or after such episodes."

Whether or not one is convinced by the work of the geneticists one point that Kallman (1953) makes is worth noting. He argues against the tendency to identify human genetics with a fatalistic outlook which would discourage therapeutic activity. He maintains that inheritability is not at all inconsistent with symptomatic treatment. He suggests that a polydactylous hand or a cleft palate may be rendered normal by operation whereas a gangrenous foot may not respond to surgery. He points out that "the effect of anticonvulsant drugs is virtually independent of the etiological type of epilepsy treated. Similarly, the knowledge that diabetus mellitus is usually inherited has not interfered with the discovery of insulin or its clinical usefulness." He argues further that a rational therapy for many hereditary conditions—including presumably psychiatric ones—may not be discovered until it is clearly determined how the genetically controlled factors are transmitted, reproduced and brought into play.

3. PSYCHOLOGICAL PREDISPOSING FACTORS

Turning from hereditary and constitutional to psychological predisposing factors, we find that the literature provides an abundance of speculations and observations, most of them in considerable agreement with one another. There have, however, been a few points of controversy. Ever since Abraham (1924) first described a "primal depression" occurring in childhood as the result of early disappointments in the child's relationship with his parents, "before the Oedipus wishes have been overcome", writers have consistently subscribed to the idea that the predisposition to depression is formed very early in childhood.

Jacobson, among the more orthodox contributors to the theory of depression, has perhaps given the most detailed exposition of the conditions allegedly necessary for the development of depressive feelings. She has described how an optimal level of self-esteem develops "only in an atmosphere of parental love and care with sufficient libidinous gratification." In such an atmosphere manageable quantities of frustration and disappointment tend to promote the process of self-discovery and reality-testing, to throw the child back on his own resources and to facilitate the establishment of solid endopsychic boundaries between self- and object-images. Such an atmosphere gradually allows the child to learn to tolerate his own ambivalence and is conducive to the establishment of a realistic ego ideal and a maturely self-critical superego.

She moreover has focused attention on the importance of severe early disappointments in the development of depressed patients. She defines disappointment as the experience that results from non-fulfillment of expectations of gratification from an object. In other words she labels as disappointment the feeling that a child has when he fails to get the affection and love and other gratifications that he is expecting. Now in some measure this is the fate of every human child. And small quantities of disappointment, coming at a time when the child has developed sufficiently to tolerate these deprivations, are indispensable in helping the child learn about the limitations of his own and his parents' omnipotence. Disappointments and frustrations in manageable doses help him to evaluate the world more realistically. It is as if small doses of disappointment in an optimal setting are useful in immunizing the child against the much larger doses of disappointment, anxiety and frustration that he is bound to be exposed to later in life.

But Jacobson emphasizes that the child who has been disappointed too massively and too early in life cannot profit from his experience. Instead he sustains a deep narcissistic injury. This narcissistic injury corresponds to the feeling of being unvalued, unwanted and unloved. The child thus sets up inside himself the judgment of his parents concerning him. In other words, he develops a harsh and critical superego. Furthermore, this narcissistic injury occurring before the child has learned how to tolerate his ambivalence interferes with the optimal cathexis of self- and object-representations, i.e., with the development of normal self-esteem and satisfactory interpersonal relationships.

Immoderate frustrations experienced too early may also interfere with the establishment of adequate boundaries between the self- and object-images and between these and the ego ideal. The magical idealized omnipotent components of the pre-oedipal ego ideal remain prominent and in later life the patient has to live up to this exaggerated ego ideal before he can experience satisfactory self-esteem. Whitehorn (1952) has drawn particular attention to the depressed patient's excessive demands upon himself. He points out that these patients "have characteristically been demanding of themselves and of others a very extreme degree of self-control, amounting, in effect, to omnipotence. Failing in the omnipotent control of themselves or of events, they feel guilty and insecure."

Thus in summary, Jacobson attributes the predisposition to depression to the occurrence of excessive disappointments at a time before the child has learned how to handle his ambivalent feelings towards himself and his love-objects and at a time when the endopsychic representations of his self and his objects have not yet been firmly established or distinguished.

Among the other writers on depression it is only Melanie Klein (1934, 1940) who offers an equally sweeping and general hypothesis to explain the predisposition to depressed states. She too emphasizes the importance of the infant's coming to terms with his own feelings of ambivalence in the process of his personality development. Her theory centers around the child's attempt to achieve satisfactory object relationships in the presence of conflicting feelings of love and of hate. The infant is believed by Melanie Klein to enter a phase which is characterized by a complex mixture of feelings consisting chiefly of grief and sorrow over the feared loss of his love object, a state of affairs which he attributes to his own greedy hostility and because of which he feels guilty and self-reproachful. The period when the child experiences this combination of guilt and fear and sorrow and self-reproach is called by her "the depressive position." She believes that those infants who fail to pass successfully through this so-called depressive position remain liable to succumb to this same set of depressive feelings again and again throughout their lives.

It is in this period, Melanie Klein believes, that the infant must come to terms with the realization that the object that he hates, the "bad object," and the object that he loves, the "good object," are in reality one person, a "whole object." This depressive position is believed by her to be characterized by fears on the part of the child that his hatred and aggression will prove stronger than his love and will result in the lasting loss of his object. Melanie Klein believes that in a favorable outcome the child becomes confident of his mother's love for him and of his own capacity to love, i.e., he succeeds in establishing his "good objects" securely within his ego. She postulates that a predisposition to depression arises only if the infant fails to establish his loved object within his ego, i.e., only if he fails to develop feelings of trust and belief in his objects and in his own capacity to love.

There has been considerable opposition in the psychoanalytic literature (e.g., Glover, 1945) to the concept of a "normal" infantile depressive position. Melanie Klein's contention has often been misunderstood to mean that every infant goes through a psychotic depressive episode in the course of his development. Zetzel (1953) has helped to clarify Melanie Klein's hypothesis. She understands it to refer simply to "the growth of object relationships in an ambivalent setting." More specifically she suggests that Melanie Klein is referring to a phase through which every infant must pass, the weaning process. She feels that Melanie Klein "is offering the hypothesis that the attainment of a predominantly positive object relationship prior to this first object loss is crucial for future development. The infant, that is to say, during the weaning process must come to terms with a real object loss—i.e., the breast or its substitute. This is the basis for the concept of a 'depressive position.' "

Therese Benedek (1956) describes "a significant variation in the primary psychic organization" which sounds very analogous to Melanie Klein's "depressive position" and which she terms the "depressive constellation." She too considers this to be of "a universal nature" and to represent the "intensification of the hostile-aggressive component of the ambivalent core in the child." She feels that in later life specific stresses may reactivate this "universal core organization" and produce a depression. Benedek believes that an infant can best be protected against a psychological accentuation of the depressive constellation by "confidence" developing through multiple repetitions of gratifying nursing experiences. "Confidence" as she uses the term, is analogous with Melanie Klein's conception of the introjection of good objects.

Melanie Klein's picture of the infant's eventual achievement of self-esteem and satisfactory object relationships in the midst of conflicting feelings of hate and love bears an obvious resemblance to Jacobson's theory of how these same goals are achieved. And despite the marked difference in terminology there are perhaps more basic conceptual similarities than differences in their theoretical outlines of this process even though Jacobson goes far beyond Melanie Klein in her discussion of the intermediate steps of this development. Nevertheless they differ to some extent in their conceptions of how the infant may fail to achieve a state of good object relationships and adequate self-esteem. Jacobson speaks of excessive disappointments experienced too early thus bringing into consideration the effect of the quality of the parent-child relationship on the development of the child. She, as Zetzel (1953) points out, "postulates an identification with these devalued useless parents, leading to diminution of the ego and the sense of worthlessness so characteristic of the depressive. She would . . . .regard the precipitating event in this pathogenic chain of events as emanating from some real failure on the part of the parents." On the other hand, Melanie Klein, while not disregarding the actual behavior of the parents would tend to attribute the child's depressive reaction to his feeling that all goodness and love and security are lost, "and lost as a result of his own uncontrollable greedy and destructive phantasies and impulses against his mother's breasts" (Klein, 1934). In other words, according to Melanie Klein, the child attributes the disappointing parental behavior mainly to his own excessive greed and sadism.

Most writers are content to refer vaguely to the pre-oedipal period as the one in which predisposition to depression is formed, and by this period they mean the first few years of life. Melanie Klein (1948) differs with this view on two counts. She considers the critical period to be as early as the first few months of life; and she refers to this period not as pre-oedipal but as indeed already oedipal. She postulates that the infant is at this time already experiencing oedipal fantasies. Moreover, she considers that these fantasies, or these early introjects as she would refer to them, are derived from the mother's breast and the father's penis about which the infant is already presumed to have some conceptualizations.

Zetzel (1953) suggests that Melanie Klein arrived at this controversial conclusion because in her clinical work with children she found superego-like introjections preceding the classical oedipal period and instead of considering that precursors of the superego antedate the oedipal period, chose to conclude that the oedipus complex antedates the genital level. However, outside the so-called English school of psychoanalysis, there is almost complete disagreement with Melanie Klein on the theoretical implications of these clinical observations. Be that as it may, she believes that it is these early months of life culminating around the period of weaning that are decisive in determining whether or not a predominantly good object has been successfully introjected, i.e., whether or not a depressive predisposition has been averted.

Most (but not all) of these speculations about predisposition to depression are retroactively derived from the study of adult patients. However, there is in addition an abundance of clinical evidence in the literature (see Bowlby, 1952) to document in a general way the pathological effects on personality development of severe deprivations in early childhood. Valuable and pertinent as these observations are, they are not to be viewed as evidence in support of any one particular psychogenic theory as opposed to another.

In the first place, although retrospective (e.g., Bowlby, 1944; Bender, 1947) and follow-up studies of severely deprived children (Lowrey, 1940, Goldfarb, 1945) have clearly demonstrated the pathological effects of such early experiences on these children, these effects have mainly turned out to be of the schizophrenic or psychopathic variety rather than manic-depressive in type. No follow-up study, as far as the reviewer is aware, has included enough depressives to warrant drawing any conclusions from it.

Secondly, although some workers, (e.g., Spitz, 1946) have shown that early deprivations produce depressive conditions in childhood, it must be borne in mind that the word "depressed" in these cases was used in a behavioristic sense since the children under observation were still preverbal. Whether these reactions actually correspond to adult depressive states is still, at best, uncertain.

Thirdly, as Rochlin (1953a) points out, the psychotic or atypical children that have been recently described in the literature by Rank (1949), Geleerd (1949), Mahler (1952) and others can not be said to have regressed to this psychotic phase as adult psychotics are presumed to do. They have actually never developed beyond it and therefore can not strictly be compared to adult manic-depressives and schizophrenics. Although they dramatically demonstrate, in a general way, the effects of very severe early deprivation, they can hardly be used as evidence to support any one particular current theory as opposed to another, about predisposition to manic-depressive psychosis or to any other depressive reaction.

4. THE CENTRAL ANXIETY SITUATION IN HUMAN DEVELOPMENT

It was mentioned previously that Melanie Klein (1940) referred to the depressive position with its mixture of guilt and fear and sorrow and longing as the central anxiety situation in human development, "the deepest source of the painful conflicts . . . . in the child's relation to people in general." The conception of this complex of feelings as the central anxiety situation in human development warrants examination in considerable more detail.

Fairbairn (1952), another British writer whose views are in large measure related to Melanie Klein's, agrees basically with her conception of the depressive position as a composite of feelings which the infant experiences as the result of inevitable frustrations sustained at the hands of his love-objects. Like Melanie Klein, he sees this position as made up of feelings of lovelessness and unhappiness infused with anger towards the love-object and guilt and fear over this anger. He sees the great problem of the depressive individual, the individual who has never resolved the difficulties of the depressive position, as how to love without destroying by hate. In every love relationship into which such an individual enters, there is always the danger that the inevitable frustrations will arouse such feelings of rage and destruction that the relationship will be threatened. Fairbairn differs somewhat, as will be seen below, from Melanie Klein in his conception of the schizoid position, the developmental phase which, he believes, precedes the depressive position. But, like Melanie Klein, he attributes to these infantile "positions" or states of feeling, a very central importance in all neurosis. He feels that these states are not defenses "but have all the characteristics of conditions against which the ego utilizes paranoid, obsessive, hysterical and phobic techniques." In other words, he feels that the depressive and the schizoid positions are the two fundamental dangers against which all neurotic phenomena and character traits are defenses.

Michael Balint (1952) in an interesting paper examines the depressive position with its mixture of paranoid and depressive anxieties and dissects it even further into purer elements. He regularly observed that many of his patients in analysis pass through a phase

of suspicion and mistrust of what they see as a careless, loveless, indifferent environment. If they can be helped out of this paranoid
position, he noted that another state develops during which "there
is the feeling of a deep, painful, narcissistic wound which, as a rule,
can be made conscious without serious difficulty, somehow in this
way: It is terrifying and dreadfully painful that *I am not loved for
what I am,* time and time again I cannot avoid seeing that people
are critical of me; it is an irrefutable fact that no one loves me as I
want to be loved." Balint identifies this set of feelings with Melanie Klein's depressive position, although he differs from her in not
considering (at least not explicitly and as far as the writer could
determine, not implicitly) the depressive position as, in part, reactive to previous sadistic fantasies. He does not give these depressive anxieties quite the central position in all psychic phenomena
that Klein does but nevertheless agrees with her that they give rise
to a variety of defenses and reactions.

It is interesting to note that other writers with superficially quite
different theoretical approaches also speak of affective states which,
although described differently, bear certain obvious resemblances
to the depressive position, in that they are described as being in one
sense or another "basic" or "central". Karen Horney (1936), for
example, had the concept of a "basic anxiety" which, she believes,
plays a fundamental role in neurosis and which "underlies all relationships to people." This basic anxiety consists of an all-pervasive
feeling of being lonely, helpless and unlovable in a hostile world.
This fundamental anxiety was seen by Horney as being "inseparably
interwoven" with a basic hostility.

Sullivan (1942) too speculated with regard to a central core of
anxieties around which the personality structure is built and which
neurotic techniques help to keep from awareness. "The self," he
believed, "comes into being as a dynamism to preserve the feeling
of security." He went on to say that "from the disappointments in
the very early stages of life outside the womb—in which all things
were given—comes the beginning of the vast development of actions, thoughts, foresights, and so on, which are calculated to protect one from a feeling of insecurity and helplessness in the situation
which confronts one." This precariously acquired self-esteem which
Sullivan considered so important, and which corresponds largely

to the introjected good objects of Melanie Klein, is referred to by Silverberg (1952) in his attempted synthesis of Sullivanian and Freudian thought as "the psychic equivalent of somatic survival." This bears a striking resemblance to Klein's statement (1934) that "the preservation of the good object is regarded as synonymous with the survival of the ego."

We find therefore a common area of agreement among writers of many different persuasions that there is a "central anxiety position," a "basic anxiety" or whatever it is called "against which the ego requires to be defended" and which consists of the "feeling of sorrow for the loved objects, the fears of losing them and the longing to regain them," "the irrefutable fact that no one loves me as I want to be loved," the feeling that comes from being unloved, and of being alone and helpless in a hostile world. This is, in other words, the lack of self-esteem which is the result of the reflected appraisal of the early love objects.

These concepts are by no means identical, but underlying all of them is the overwhelmingly acknowleged importance of the quality of early object relationships in the type of character structure that evolves.

Glover (1945), in his comprehensive critique of the Kleinian body of theory, disputes the central importance in neurosogenesis of this depressive position and feels that it is contrary to Freud's view. It will be helpful to look at Freud's own words on the subject of what neurosis defends against.

In *The Problem of Anxiety* (1936) a comparatively late formulation of his theory, he described anxiety as a danger signal, i.e., a signal that a situation of danger was impending. This danger situation, as he conceived it, was the danger of losing the object. He amplified this concept when he remarked that "grief is therefore the reaction specific to object loss, anxiety to the danger which this object loss entails, or, by a further displacement, to the danger of the object loss itself." In this view, "all symptom formation would be brought about solely in order to avoid anxiety; the symptoms bind the psychic energy which otherwise would be discharged as anxiety, so that anxiety would be the fundamental phenomenon and the central problem of neurosis."

However, Freud went on to say that object loss took different forms at different stages of development. In early childhood he conceived of the danger as simply object loss itself, i.e., loss of the mother. But in the phallic phase, as is well known, he thought of this danger as a castration danger. At first glance it might be difficult to reconcile this with the danger of object loss but as he looked at it, "the high narcissistic value attaching to the penis may be referable to the fact that the possession of this organ contains a guaranty of reunion with the mother (or mother substitute) in the act of coitus. Deprivation of this mother . . . . has again the significance . . . . of being delivered over helpless to the unpleasurable tension arising from non-gratification of a need." The danger of object loss in the latency period was formulated by Freud as "the anger, the punishment, of the superego, the loss of its love, which the ego apprehends as a danger and to which it responds with the signal of anxiety," a view with which we are very familiar.

Thus Freud conceived of anxiety, "the central problem of neurosis" as but a signal of the real danger, the danger of loss of the object as it is experienced in its various forms in the different phases of development. Obviously this Freudian view of anxiety and the danger of object loss should not be twisted into too close a correspondence with the views outlined above, but the writer suggests that there are more than superficial resemblances to these theories in Freud's progressively increasing conceptualization of the central problem in neurosis as the danger of the loss of the actual and introjected love objects.

To summarize this section briefly, we have seen that many writers, primarily British, have observed clinically a set of intensely painful feelings of sorrow and loss and unlovableness fused with hate and guilt that they have variously termed "depressive anxieties" or "position" or "state" and which they have felt to be, not a defense, but a fundamental danger situation against which defenses and restitutive measures must be mobilized. These writers further maintained: (a) that every infant went through such a state of depressive anxieties (if he successfully passed through the variously described preceding persecutory or schizoid state); (b) that the infant's further development and proneness to depression depended on how successfully he "worked through" this position, this working through process being characterized by firmly establishing the good objects within himself, i.e., in becoming confident of love and security.

Furthermore there was surprisingly widespread agreement that the central danger position, with regard to which anxiety was a signal and neurosis a defense, was this set of depressive anxieties which were variously termed but which all had to do with the loss of the object, external or internalized and with the associated feelings of helplessness, unlovableness, desolation and lack of self-esteem.

What can be said of these attempts to attribute central importance in normal and neurotic development to one or another of these developmental problems, whether it be the depressive position of Klein or the Oedipus complex of Freud? Is one more important than the other or is the whole controversy a pseudo-problem, a perfectionistic and unrealistic attempt to assign critical priority to one of several crucial life phases, each of which is of overwhelming importance at some particular period in life? To the reviewer, it would appear that the developing infant and child has many developmental crises to weather. He has to come to terms with his own ambivalence. He has to face the problem of acquiring a rewarding and satisfying relationship with his first love-object with its implications for self-esteem and confidence. He has to attain an effective mastery over his physiological processes and his developing ego functions. He has to arrive at a solution of the "three-body relationship," as Rickman (1951) refers to it, the fateful oedipal situation which is so important in determining his subsequent ability to lead a gratifying emotional and sexual life. The growing child is confronted with the task of solving the problems of jealousy and envy that are also connected with sibling rivalry. Nor is that all. As we all know and as Sullivan (1953), and Erikson (1950) have shown, the problems of adolescence are by no means negligible in their relevance to the development of the individual.

Are any of these stages or problems or periods the most important? Or would it not be more reasonable to think of these as nodal points in human development, the successful mastery of each being largely dependent upon the degree of success in coping with previous phases? After all, one who has not successfully mastered the tensions of unrestrained ambivalence can hardly integrate the most satisfying kind of object relationship. And one who has never successfully solved the problems of the "two-body relationship" will be at a disadvantage in engaging in the conflicts of the oedipal situation. It is clear that each phase in life is colored and influenced by the previous life experiences of the individual.

This is not to suggest that there are not critical phases and important nodal points in human development. One need not subscribe to a strictly monistic theory of neurotic causation to appreciate the key importance of several of the phases and several of the problems of psychological development. The achievement of a good relationship with the mother is one of these phases, and the struggle to attain a measure of self-esteem is one of these problems. And needless to say, the satisfactory working through of the oedipal situation is one of the critical tasks of the developing child.

It is interesting to note in this connection that Gitelson (1952) in his comments on opening the symposium on the re-evaluation of the Oedipus complex at the Seventeenth International Psychoanalytic Congress stressed the importance of pre-genital conflicts. He felt that it was only on the basis of a satisfactory mother-child relationship that an individual could enter into and solve the problems of the oedipal period. He drew attention to the presence of so many borderline patients in current analytic practice who far from being able to deal with oedipal problems have never even successfully solved the problems of the primary mother-child constellation. Implying then that one who has begun to cope with the oedipal situation has already travelled a very considerable distance along the pathway of development, he significantly concluded that "the Oedipus complex thus has apical importance not so much as the nucleus of the neuroses but as the nucleus of normal character structure and as the basis of mature life."

5. OBSESSIONAL CHARACTER STRUCTURE

We will now consider the obsessional character structure that has been attributed to the depressive person in his "free intervals" by various writers. It was Abraham who first made this correlation. After having made previous observations to the effect that the obsessional neurotic and the manic-depressive had in common a marked ambivalence towards their love-objects, Abraham (1924)

stated that the manic-depressive patient "is found to have an abnormal character-formation during his 'free interval' and that this
character-formation coincides in a quite unmistakable way with that
of the obsessional neurotic." He found in his manic-depressive
patients during their non-psychotic periods the same attitudes about
cleanliness, order, money and possessions and the same defiance
and obstinacy alternating with docility and submissiveness that he
observed in obsessional neurotics.

Rado (1928) confirmed the presence of obsessional traits in
the character of melancholics between attacks. He thought of them
as reaction formations serving the purpose of psychic bulwarks for
the restraint of ambivalence and as devices to "minister to narcissistic gratification" by draining off aggressive energy into socially
acceptable channels.

Gero (1936) objected to the conceptualization of the obsessional
character as the sum of isolated qualities such as order, cleanliness,
etc. He felt that in order to understand this character structure
properly it was necessary to see these different traits in a more comprehensive and unified way. Unlike Rado, who tended to think of
obsessional traits as devices to drain off aggressive energy into useful channels, and in this sense, a healing mechanism, Gero thought
of them collectively as simply a defense, in itself part of the neurosis.
He regarded the obsessional character structure as a defense designed to guard against the coming into awareness of hostile impulses and thoughts, and a defense, moreover, which must be
analyzed immediately so that the patient's warded off impulses
could become conscious and be experienced and so that changes
could then occur.

He regarded this type of defense as "a continuous state of being
on one's guard against oneself, a complete inability to break loose.
Such people's typical reactions are mistrust of themselves and an
incapacity to let themselves go. Their impulses are always reined
in. They feel in themselves something excessive and passionate
which they fear without knowing what it is. They are afraid to lose
control lest these dark passions should carry them away. We know
that above all it is the abnormal sadistic impulses that render these
defensive measures necessary. These patients suffer from a chronic
damming up of the feeling of aggression. On the one hand their re-

pressed feelings of aggression are tremendously strong, on the other hand their excessively strict superego does not permit them even innocent acts of aggression. Always held back, continually hurt, they long for revenge, but they can never satisfy these feelings." However it must be noted that his case material led Gero to question the universality of this type of character structure in depressed patients.

Stengel, who has reported extensively on the association of obsessional neurosis with psychotic reaction types (1945, 1946) states quite categorically (1948): "I do not agree with those writers who maintain that the typical features of the obsessional character can be found in every case of manic-depressive illness."

Edith Jacobson's (1953) case material also leads her to question the thesis that the manic-depressive shows obsessive or compulsive traits during his free intervals. She finds that even during these intervals there are vacillations in mood and efficiency that are not at all characteristic of compulsives. Neither is there in the cyclothymic patient the independence which exists in the compulsive and which is the result of the latter's dependence on his own superego for self-esteem. She finds that the manic-depressive does, at times, lean on his superego. This, it is true, gives him the appearance of independence. However this is illusory since he also simultaneously or alternately depends upon some idealized love-object which, she feels, does not happen in the true compulsive.

Mabel Blake Cohen and her co-workers (1954), in their study of manic-depressive psychosis, also feel that there are important differences between the manic-depressive character and the obsessional character, although they focus attention on rather different aspects of the obsessional character than Jacobson does. The main difference that they see is that the manic-depressive has a marked lack of interpersonal awareness which makes him overlook the particular characteristics and qualities of the other person, whereas the obsessional, although hostile, controlling and envious, does nevertheless have an awareness of the other person as a person.

Attention must be drawn to the observation that all of these judgments refer specifically to manic-depressive patients and not to other kinds of depressives. There seem to be hardly any comparable psychoanalytic references to other groups of depressed patients with data relevant to this aspect of their character structure. However, as was indicated in an earlier chapter, several clinical psychiatric studies (Titley, 1936; Palmer and Sherman, 1938; Malamud and Sands, 1941) seem to show that the obsessional character structure is much more typical of the prepsychotic involutional melancholic than of the prepsychotic manic-depressive.

6. AGGRESSION IN DEPRESSION

Concern with the obsessional character is in large part concern with the defenses of the depressed or depression-prone person. But psychoanalytic writers have been even more concerned with the impulses against which these defenses operate. The most important of these impulses is aggression.

Abraham (1911) first noted the presence of hostility and ambivalence in the psychopathology of the depressive. Freud (1917) gave classical expression to this theme in his interpretation of the meaning of the melancholic's self-reproaches. He saw these self-reproaches as hostile feelings which the patients unconsciously felt towards their love-objects and which, with the abandonment of these objects, they had redirected towards their own persons with which the objects had now become identified. Abraham (1924) later provided clinical documentation of these observations.

Rado (1928) later also supported Freud's conception of the depressive's hostility and reported an irritability and embittered rebelliousness in depressives even before the so-called melancholic introjection. From this time the theme of aggression was a central one in psychoanalytic writing on depression. It was a theme that was particularly emphasized by Melanie Klein (1948). Her view of a Death Instinct as innate in every person from birth onwards influenced her to assign even greater emphasis to the alleged association of hostility and aggression with every depressive reaction. She conceives of the infant as turning the self-directed aggressive energy of the Death Instinct outwards and reacting to frustration with hostile, sadistic feelings. Indeed she has labelled as the "depressive position" that phase in human development when the infant can allegedly feel guilt and sorrow over the feared loss of the love-object which it attributes to its own sadistic impulses. She believes that this depressive position is the prototype for all clinical depressions, and the concept of hostility and aggression is thus for her intimately bound up with the concept of depression.

The association of aggression and depression has become so common in psychoanalytic and general psychiatric thinking that it is of interest to find four writers who have challenged the universality of this association. Balint (1952), for example, utilizes the concept of a depressive position and yet, unlike Klein, sees it as free of aggressive coloring. He conceives of a pre-ambivalent infantile state which he calls the period of archaic object love. The depressive position follows the loss of this state and he speaks of it in terms of "a deep painful narcissistic wound." Despite Balint's thesis that such an infantile state exists, he refers to bitterness and resentment about an undeserved injury as occurring "in every form of depression" but speaks of these feelings as secondary narcissistic features. He considers them reactions to, rather than essential elements of, depression.

Bibring (1953) also regarded aggression as a secondary phenomenon and as not necessarily a component part of every depression. He stated that "it seems justified to generalize that the turning of aggressive impulses against the self is secondary to a breakdown of the self-esteem . . . . However there are depressions which are not accompanied by any self-aggression and there are cases of angry self-hatred which do not show any manifest signs of depression."

He was echoed in these remarks by Cohen and her colleagues (1953) who say about their patients' hostility: "We feel that it has been considerably overstressed as a dynamic factor in the illness." They would relegate the hostility that does appear to a secondary position. "We see hostile feelings arising in the patient as the result of frustration of his manipulative and exploitative needs . . . . But we feel that much of the hostility that has been imputed to the patient has been the result of his annoying impact upon others, rather than of a primary motivation to do injury to them."

Gero (1953) challenges the view that all self-devaluation can be considered self-directed aggression. In a patient whom he was treating, one kind of self-devaluation and self-dissatisfaction was not, according to him, a superego reaction (i.e., a manifestation of aggression) but "the expression of a perception based on the withdrawal of libidinal cathexis from the genital region and secondarily from the whole body." In other words, this particular patient's complaints about the ugliness of her body was characterized as "a generalized feeling of being castrated," a statement of grief.

Thus, as we can see, there appear to be radical differences of opinion about the role of aggression in the depressive reactions. However, a review of the pertinent literature reveals the presence of two semantic and conceptual difficulties which contribute a very considerable share to the theoretical difficulties we have been discussing.

The first of these difficulties has to do with the definition of depression, the second with the definition of aggression. The first difficulty is the easiest to resolve for it is largely a question of definition. Some authors require the presence of aggression for the diagnosis of depression. It is therefore hardly surprising that they find it. Indeed, were they not to find aggression they would be forced, as Beres (1958) has acknowledged, to deny that the illness was depression. The two leading exponents of this viewpoint are Jacobson and Fairbairn. For Jacobson, depression and the vicissitudes of aggression are inseparable. In the more psychotic depressions she sees a massive redirection of hostile feelings from the object to the self-image. In other depressions there may be a less explicit deployment of aggressive energy between the ego and the ego ideal with accompanying feelings of unworthiness, inadequacy or inferiority. In still other depressions which are characterized by feelings of guilt and moral unworthiness, the aggressive tension is between the superego and the ego.

Those states which other writers refer to as depressions and which consist primarily of feelings of loneliness and longing are not considered by Jacobson to be depressions at all. She acknowledges (1957) that these states are mostly free of aggressive elements and that they are often characterized primarily by the lack of gratification of libidinal impulses.

For Fairbairn (1952) too, depression is intimately associated with aggression. However he believes that there is an earlier and more basic reaction than anger to the loss of the object. This he calls not "depression" but the "schizoid" way of reacting. Patients who react in this way to object loss will frequently describe themselves as being depressed. However, when they describe what they mean by depression they will use such words as "lonely," "empty", "a feeling of futility," "feeling out of touch," "hungry," etc. There is frequently no communication or indication of guilt or anger —just a sad, empty loneliness that appears quite different in quality from the retarded depression of the cyclothymic person. Since Fairbairn believes that there is no element of anger in this reaction, he excludes it from the category of depression.

The second semantic difficulty to which we have referred has to do with the various meanings assigned to the concept of "aggression." In the first place, "aggression" may be used either as a description of behavior or as an explanation of behavior with no clear distinction between these two uses. In the second place "aggression" may be used either for impulses or feelings or for a highly abstract concept of psychic energy, again with little distinction between these uses.

René Spitz provides an example of these difficulties. In his paper, "Anaclitic Depression" (1946), he attempts to make this type of depression conform to the mechanism which Freud (1917) postulated in "Mourning and Melancholia." He declares that "in the infant the superego is absent, so that it is impossible to assume destructive hostility of the superego. However, the loss of the love object in itself is equivalent to a hostile deprivation for the infant." The infants that he studied were restricted in their locomotion and thus blocked from making contact with other children or adults. "Inhibited in its motor release, the pent-up aggressive drive is turned against the ego." The manifestation of this self-directed aggression is assumed, in conformity with Freud's theory about melancholics, to be the anaclitic depression itself. Here Spitz resorts to the concept of a retroflexed aggressive drive to provide an explanation for the anaclitic depression primarily on the basis of accepted theory, rather than on the basis of observable behavior.

In his later paper (1953), Spitz uses the term in an additional way. He postulates that in the infant in the second half of the first year, the libidinal and the aggressive drives are both directed towards the same object. He believes that if this object is removed from the infant, the aggressive drive, for a time, finds no target. "It is the relationship with the love object which gives the infant the opportunity to release its aggressive drives . . . . If the infant is deprived of the libidinal object, both drives are deprived of their target. This is what happened to the infants affected with anaclitic depression . . . . If we follow the fate of the aggressive drive, we find these infants slowly becoming self-destructive. It is in such cases that we have found the frequent manifestations of headbanging."

Spitz goes on to remark that infants, after regaining their libidinal object and after recovering from their depression, become even more aggressive against others than normal children of their age. It is inferred from this externally-directed aggression which occurs in the period of recovery from depression that previously, during the depressed state, this aggression must have been directed inwards. Spitz suggests this when he remarks that "after coming out of the anaclitic depression the restored infant no longer hits or scratches itself. It now begins to bite, to scratch, to kick others."

In both of these latter two examples, Spitz seems to be speaking in a far more behavioristic sense when referring to aggression. He no longer theorizes that the depression itself is simply the manifestation of self-directed aggression. When he speaks of the aggression turned against the self, or against others, he refers to observable self-destruction, or aggression towards others, rather than to a hypothetical drive.

We have noted that a second confusion in the use of the term "aggression" is occasioned by the failure to distinguish between aggression as an impulse or feeling and aggression as a highly abstract concept of psychic energy. This confusion is well illustrated in the use of the term by Jacobson. When a manic-depressive abandons his love-object and withdraws into a psychotic depression, for example, she postulates that all of the hostility that he had felt towards the object becomes experienced as directed against the self, since, by a regressive dissolution of identifications, the object- and self-images have merged.

This manner of deploying aggressive energy is quite different from what she presumes to happen to an individual who fails in some way to live up to his ego ideal. Here she considers that the superego cathects the self-image with aggressive energy and that self-esteem drops. But the objects are still retained and there is no massive withdrawal of libidinal cathexis from them. In such a case, it would not seem correct to say that the aggression meant for an object has now been redirected or retroflexed. The aggressive energy with which the self-representation is cathected to bring about the drop in self-esteem is certainly related to the original disapproval experienced by the individual from his parents. According to the theory, his superego has taken over their role. But this aggressive energy with which his self-image is now presumed to be cathected is a much less positively identifiable affective entity than the hostility which the manic-depressive feels for his disappointing object and which he reflexes on himself. To speak of both of these situations simply as manifestations of aggression would seem only to confuse the issue.

Hartmann (1955) has made an attempt to conceptualize the manner in which various manifestations of aggression are related to one another. It had long been considered that libidinal energy is transformed into non-sexual energy and made available to the ego for non-sexual purposes. This transformation is referred to as "sublimation." Hartmann suggests that a similar transformation occurs with aggressive energy, a transformation that he terms "neutralization." He further proposes that the word "neutralization" be used in a general sense to refer not only to the deaggressivization of aggressive energy but also to the desexualization or sublimation of libidinal energy. Moreover he thinks "it comes closer to observable facts to speak . . . . not just of two modes of energy of each drive: instinctual or neutralized. Both clinical experience and theory point to the probability that there exists a continuum of gradations of energy, from the fully instinctual to the fully neutralized mode." In this connection he speaks of the aggression that the superego uses in its relations to the ego as being already partly modified from its purely hostile, destructive "instinctual mode."

The dangers inherent in this reification of energy have been critically considered by Kubie (1947) and a recent conference on psychiatric education (Whitehorn, 1953) has warned against taking seriously "any applied identity or too close analogy with the concepts of energy, tension or pressure in the sense that the physicist uses these terms."

As the reader can see, the study of the theoretical models constructed to help understand the depressive reactions sometimes carries one into regions that can most charitably be described as metapsychological. It is in this particular aspect of the depressive problem that one most frequently encounters a level of discourse far removed from clinical reality. Freud's explanation of the melancholic's self-reproaches and Abraham's description of the manic-depressive's ambivalence became universally, and, it is feared, uncritically and uniformly applied to all depressive phenomena. And later authors frequently sought to justify these constructions rather than to investigate their applicability.

In summary, there is very little consensus in the literature on the relation of aggression to depression. There is no agreement as to whether aggression is an innate primary human drive or whether it appears only secondarily in reaction to frustration — or indeed as to whether this antithesis has any real meaning. There is no agreement as to whether or not aggression is related to a hypothetical Death Instinct. There is no agreement as to whether aggression is central to the problem of depression or secondary. And there has been very little notice paid to the various ways in which the word "aggression" is used. In short, speculation is rife, consensus minimal and confusion distressingly common.

7. ORALITY IN DEPRESSION

Let us now turn to an examination of the theories about the presence of "orality" in depression. Abraham (1916), in corroboration of Freud's (1910) original formulation about the role of the erogenous zones in psychosexual development, provided numerous clinical examples of patients whose mode of achieving libidinal gratification was by stimulation of their oral zone. He theorized that oral eroticism in neurotic depressives has two functions: to prevent an episode of depression and to remove one once it has occurred. He reported one depressed patient who was inexplicably soothed by drinking a cup of milk that his mother brought him. Abraham further postulated that the melancholically depressed patient regresses in his unconscious to the oral phase of psychosexual development and that he directs upon his love-object the wish to incorporate it, a wish that is colored by hostility so that it is simultaneously a desire to devour and to demolish the object. Abraham felt that it was the guilt associated with this hostile cannibalistic wish that accounted for the melancholic's refusal to take food and for his fear of starvation.

Freud (1917), as we know, interpreted the melancholic's self-reproaches as being in reality directed against the abandoned love-object which had been introjected into the ego. For Freud this introjection represented a regression of libido from object choice to the earliest and original form of object relationship.

He felt that this earliest type of relationship was essentially an oral phenomenon since one of the infant's most primitive reactions to objects was to put them into his mouth. This was considered by Freud to be the earliest method of relating to an object and one which he referred to as "identification" since it represented for Freud an attempt to be magically at one with the loved object. And in what way could the infant be more at one with the loved object than by actually putting it into his mouth and incorporating it into himself?

After the abandonment of the object by the melancholic, Freud believed that it was this process that took place, namely a regression to an identification with the object by means of its introjection into the ego, the introjection being conceptualized as an oral act. And he understood the self-reproaches to be reproaches against this introjected object. He furthermore agreed with Abraham's explanation of the melancholic's refusal to eat, since he too considered this introjection of the object to be essentially an unconsciously hostile cannabilistic act. In turn Abraham (1924) attempted to corroborate Freud's hypothesis that introjection takes place by an oral mechanism by numerous clinical examples drawn from his patients' fantasies and dreams. He furthermore postulated a constitutional and inherited over-accentuation of oral eroticism in potential melancholics, i.e., an increased capacity to experience pleasures in the oral zone. He thought that as a result of this alleged constitutional intensification of oral needs and consequent oral frustrations such patients suffered a special fixation of psychosexual development at the oral level.

Rado (1928), as was mentioned earlier, performed two services to the understanding of orality. He was one of the first workers to broaden the concept of orality by trying to show "that pleasurable stimulation of the mouth-zone does not constitute the whole of the oral-libidinal gratification but should rather be regarded as its more conspicuous antecedent." He referred to the climax of the process of which the mouth pleasure was the precursor by the suggestively descriptive term, "alimentary orgasm," a term which has, by and large, failed to enter into the everyday currency of psychoanalytic language. He suggested that the pleasure which the infant experiences at his mother's breasts and which includes components of security, warmth and nourishment, is the prototype of the narcissistic gratification that is later experienced as self-satisfaction and self-esteem.

Rado argued that "the deepest fixation point in the (melancholic) depressive disposition is to be found in the . . . . hunger-situation of the infant" by which he meant that the "intensely strong craving for narcissistic gratification" which he found so characteristic of depressives had its roots in the hungry feelings of the ungratified infant. And just as the "oral-narcissistic bliss" of the infant is dependent upon supplies of nourishment from the outside, so does the narcissistic gratification of the depressive, he felt, depend upon love, appreciation and recognition by others — what Fenichel (1945) was to refer to as "external narcissistic supplies." Rado considered that the narcissistic people who are so predisposed to depression "have a sense of security and comfort only when they feel themselves loved, esteemed, supported and encouraged."

Gero (1936) made this broader interpretation of orality more explicit by dissociating it even further from its purely buccal and alimentary connotations and by extending its meaning to cover all aspects of the early mother-child relationship. "Inseparable from it is the pleasurable contact with the skin, the comfortable feeling of warmth emanating from the mother's body. . . . . The specifically oral pleasure is only one factor in the experience satisfying the infant's need for warmth, touch, love and care." It is in this wider sense that he believed that the depressive type is oral. He "longs for shelter and love, and for the warmth of the mother's protecting body."

It was Fenichel (1945) who more fully described the narcissistic oral character of the depressive, the "person who is fixated on the state where his self-esteem is regulated by external supplies." He sketched a vivid picture of the depressive's perpetual greediness, his extremely dependent need to be loved and his inordinate demands upon his love-objects. He considered that "a severe depression represents the state into which the orally dependent individual gets when the vital supplies are lacking."

In opposition to this general theoretical trend, Bibring (1953) first openly questioned the universality of oral fixation and oral orientation in depression. Since his demurral has reopened an issue that seemed for a long time to be a closed one, let us glance more carefully at the issue of oral fixation in depression.

The alleged orality of depressives seems to have three theoretical and historical sources. In the first place, it has long been pointed out that depressives have oral fantasies and are inclined to oral gratifications. About this, Jacobson (1953) says, "It has seemed to me to be of lesser importance [than other factors that she emphasizes] that the melancholic divulges cannibalistic incorporation and anal-sadistic ejection fantasies. All psychotics, schizophrenic or manic-depressives manifest such deeply regressive id material." Thus she indicates that such fantasies are by no means characteristic of depression.

Glover (1955) moreover points out that one should guard against being misled by the mere presence of oral manifestations. He feels that they may actually represent a defensive regression to cope with the "anxieties connected with a later fixation point." He reports, for example, two cases, examples of "lesser depressive states," in which "the oral constructions represented only a defensive regression from an Oedipus conflict, which by an unusual coincidence was associated in both cases with a circumcision trauma following the birth of a rival brother at an early stage of his Oedipus phase, namely almost three years of age . . . . We should always bear in mind the possibility that a seemingly deep regression may be a cover for a later fixation."

Secondly, ever since Rado (1928), writers have repeatedly described the depressive person in terms of his excessive dependence for self-esteem on external narcissistic supplies of love, affection and attention, supplies, which, by virtue of Rado's elaboration of the term, are considered to be essentially oral in character. Bibring

(1953) acknowledged that the " 'orally dependent type' which constantly needs 'narcissistic supplies' from the outside represents perhaps the most frequent type of predisposition to depression" but he denied that all persons who develop depression have this type of predisposition. As was outlined previously, Bibring's view was that "depression can be defined as the emotional correlate of a partial or complete collapse of the self-esteem of the ego, since it feels unable to live up to its aspirations." He acknowledged that some of these narcissistic aspirations ("the need to get affection, to be loved, to be taken care of," etc.) are developed or built on the oral level, though even here he stressed the point "that the emphasis is not on the oral frustration and subsequent oral fixation, but on the infant's or little child's shocklike experience of and fixation to the feeling of helplessness." However, his clinical material forced him to conclude that depressions can also occur due to the inability to live up to aspirations linked with other phases of psychosexual development, e.g., the anal ("the wish to be good, not to be resentful, defiant, but to be loving, not to be dirty," etc.) and the phallic ("the wish to be admired, to be the center of attention, to be strong or victorious," etc.).

Doubtless, an argument could be made that at bottom these latter types of aspirations are actually derived from oral needs, i.e., that one might wish to be good, clean, loving, strong, admired, etc. because one wished to be loved and taken care of or because one had to defend oneself against these needs. Actually it seems very unlikely that any depressive in treatment will not eventually produce "oral material" despite the nature of the presenting grievance. But, as was indicated above, the mere presence of oral material does not necessarily imply an oral fixation.

Be that as it may, it would seem that the value of Bibring's observation lies in his calling attention to the difference in maturity and development implied by the clinical fact that one person's equilibrium seems to be based exclusively on the attainment of narcissistic supplies from an outside love object and another's on the attainment of narcissistic supplies from an internalized source by the fulfillment of certain aspirations and ideals.

A third source of the theory of oral fixation in depression was Freud's (1917) original designation of the process that occurs in melancholia as an identification of the ego with the abandoned love-object, a process that was believed to represent a regression to "the way in which the ego first adopts an object" namely incorporation. Since this kind of emotional tie was considered to represent the type of object relationship characteristic of the earliest phase of life, and since incorporation was considered to be an oral phenomenon, Freud concluded that "among the special characteristics of melancholia (was) a regression from object-cathexis to the still narcissistic oral phase of the libido." Subsequently all depressions in which introjection or identification were believed to take place, and this particularly included psychotic depressions, were considered to be based on oral mechanisms.

However, as was seen earlier, there is considerable evidence (e.g., Fenichel, 1931, 1937) that incorporation fantasies need by no means be only oral in nature, since respiratory, anal, ocular and many other types have been described.

As to the designation of the typical melancholic restitutive mechanism as an oral phenomenon because introjection is involved, perhaps it would be more profitable to by-pass the whole thorny question of whether this phenomenon takes place by instinctual processes and to think about it as Jacobson (1953) does. She has adopted the point of view of modern ego psychology and thinks about the "pathognomonic introjection" not so much in psychosexual terms as in terms of ego mechanisms. As has been discussed, she conceptualizes the mechanism in melancholia not so much as an identification achieved through oral means but rather as a regressive dissolution of ego identifications, a "breakdown of realistic object- and self-representations, of object relations and of ego functions" in which reality testing is lost, the self-images are confused with object-representations and in which the latter no longer adequately reflect the actual objects.

8. INTROJECTIVE MECHANISMS IN DEPRESSION

To treat this subject exhaustively the reviewer should discuss in much more detail the various controversies centering around the relationship between introjection and orality and between introjection and identification. These matters have occupied the attention of numerous authors (e.g., Fuchs, 1937; Knight, 1940) and have given rise to many sophisticated attempts at definition and differentiation. The present writer will however refrain from attempting to review fully this confusing theoretical issue except to indicate that Jacobson (1954b) uses the term "introjection" in a manner quite different from that of any of her predecessors.

In her quest for terminological precision, she takes issue with the previous usage of the terms "introjection" and "projection." Melanie Klein (1948), for example, makes frequent references to the introjection of good and bad objects by which she means the internalization of good and bad aspects of the love-object.

Jacobson objects to giving "introjection" this vague connotation of internalization, although it must be said that this has been the meaning assigned to it in the psychoanalytic literature of even the most classic variety. Knight (1940), for example, defines introjection "as an unconscious inclusion of an object or part of an object into the ego of the subject." And Fenichel (1945) states that "introjection is an attempt to make parts of the external world flow into the ego."

Jacobson takes issue with what she regards as the terminological and conceptual imprecision of speaking of objects, rather than object-images, being included in the ego. And furthermore she (1954b) prefers to speak not of object-images being formed by a process of introjection, but less magically of object-images emerging "from the ever-increasing memory traces of pleasurable and unpleasurable experiences and of perceptions with which they become associated." By the term "introjection" she refers strictly to the endopsychic process in which the self-image assumes characteristics of the object-representations. If, according to her, object-images accurately reflect external objects, then their introjection will endow the self-representations—and the self—with attributes of real persons. She considers that in the introjective process in psychotic states the self-images assume characteristics of very archaic object-images which reflect current external reality very poorly. It is in this sense that she speaks of the mechanism in melancholia as consisting of a dissolution of ego identifications in which the object-images no longer accurately reflect actual objects and in which the self-representation, by a process of introjection, takes on the characteristics of these unrealistic object-images. In other words, the self- and object-representations, which are never at any time adequately delineated from one another in the pre-psychotic personality, according to Jacobson, now with the onset of the psychotic state, fuse and merge with one another.

Chapter V

1. INTRODUCTION

Now THAT WE HAVE examined these various aspects of the multi-faceted subject of the depressed states, it might be well to step back a pace and to consider these conditions not in the microscopic manner of the preceding pages but, instead, macroscopically, from the point of view of diagnostic entities. There has been a remarkable advance in psychiatric sophistication since the days when it was thought that there were a host of clinical entities waiting to be recognized and isolated from one another, each with its different toxic or histopathological etiology. Diagnostic entities are not now accorded quite the same respectful attention in psychiatry as they are in other medical specialties. Nor is this surprising in view of the fact that there is actually no uniform system of diagnostic classification. Some conditions are characterized on the basis of behavior in the narrower sense of the word, others on the basis of thoughts and sense perceptions while others still are classified according to the dominant mood. And the number of psychiatrists who feel that there is some absolute difference between all these various conditions is small indeed. One speaks for example not of a disease called "obsessionalism" but rather of obsessional traits in so-called normal character structure, of obsessional neuroses and of obsessional defenses against a schizophrenic or a manic-depressive breakdown. One no longer faithfully subscribes to the old clean-cut divisions between diagnostic categories. The human being and his life experiences can not always be neatly compressed into a diagnostic compartment.

It is somewhat difficult at this point in the development of psychiatry, when the emphasis is so largely and so properly on the individual patient and his problems, to become greatly concerned or even interested in fine diagnostic distinctions which sometimes appear so irrelevant to the treatment of any particular patient.

Yet, despite all this, diagnoses are the daily currency with which psychiatrists, in common with their medical colleagues, conduct their affairs. And even if this currency does not represent the pure gold of another era, neither can it be said to be entirely debased. The diagnostic categories must represent some approximation to clinical reality or else they would have gone the way of devils and humors in psychiatric thinking. Even those clinicians who focus on the motivational and experiential, in contrast with the formal and diagnostic, aspects of psychiatric illness, implicitly and explicitly acknowledge the usefulness of the clinical categories.

2. DIAGNOSTIC ASPECTS OF DEPRESSION

We have previously given some consideration to the diagnostic aspects of the depressive reactions. We have noted the controversy over whether it is possible to differentiate neurotic from psychotic depression and have indicated that psychoanalytic writers have tended to concur in this differentiation. However, there has been no absolute unanimity about whether manic-depressive psychosis does or does not represent a distinct diagnostic category. Zilboorg (1933), for instance, declares that "on the basis of my clinical experience I am under the definite impression that manic-depressive psychoses despite their age-long existence do not actually represent a separate clinical entity."

Most current psychoanalytic writers on the subject, however, acknowledge with relatively little hesitation the usefulness of this Kraepelinian category. Cohen and her colleagues (1954) for example, consider that "the manic-depressive syndrome does represent a fairly clear-cut system of defenses which are sufficiently unique and of sufficient theoretical interest to deserve separate study." And Jacobson (1953) indicates quite explicitly that she regards manic-depressive psychosis as a distinct clinical entity.

The question of whether involutional melancholia is an entity that is different from manic-depressive psychosis has been previously reviewed in these pages. It will be recalled that the consensus now is that there is indeed a difference between these conditions, a difference both in the prepsychotic personality structure and in the symptomatology of these two depressive psychoses.

Recent psychoanalytic descriptions of the prepsychotic manic-depressive personality correspond rather closely to the older clinical psychiatric pictures. Jacobson (1953), for example, mentions that before their psychoses, these patients "may be delightful companions or marital partners, a feature that Bleuler mentioned especially. In their sexual life they may show a full genital response, and emotionally . . . . a touching warmth and unusual, affectionate clinging to people they like."

This description as we have seen is markedly different from that of the prepsychotic personality of the involutional melancholic as reported by such writers as Titley (1936), Palmer and Sherman (1938) etc. However no comparable psychoanalytic studies or descriptions exist. As for the actual psychoses, Glover (1955) remarks that "involutional states represent a mixture of reactions chiefly characteristic of depression but frequently having some resemblance to maniacal and schizophrenic discharge. No *specific* conflict factors have been determined."

In view of this observation it is interesting to note that Kallman (1953), on the basis of his research in heredity, states that "the principal genetic relationship of that type of emotional instability which may lead to an involutional psychosis is (not to manic-depressive psychosis but) to the group of schizoid personality traits."

Fenichel (1945) admits that "psychoanalytically not much is known about the structure and mechanisms of involutional melancholias. They seem to occur in personalities with an outspoken character of an especially rigid nature."

This relative ignorance of involutional melancholia from the psychoanalytic point of view is only too frequently overlooked. Facile interpretations are frequently based on studies which were actually conducted on manic-depressive patients. In view of the depressive mood and the self-accusations common to both of these reactions it is not improbable that similar psychological events occur in them but the fact remains that the literature is practically—but not entirely (see Kaufman, 1937)—devoid of psychoanalytic studies of involutional melancholia.

Nor surprisingly enough can there be said to exist an impressive volume of contributions on the subject of the neurotic depressive reactions. Freud (1917) explicitly recognized the difference between neurotic and psychotic depression but preferred to concern himself chiefly with the latter. Abraham (1916) threw some incidental light on neurotic depression but also mainly addressed himself to the problem of manic-depressive psychosis. Rado (1928) indicated that the former type of depressive reaction differed from the latter chiefly in the extent of the narcissistic regression but abstained from considering in any detail what further differences, if any, existed. Bibring (1953) made some general remarks about all types of depression but provided no clinical documentation of his very plausible thesis. And Jacobson (1953) though making some very pertinent and clarifying generalizations about depression nevertheless makes it clear at several points that she is chiefly concerned with psychotic depression. It therefore happens that although it is by no means true to say that the neurotic depressive reaction has been overlooked in the literature (see especially Fenichel, 1945; Lorand, 1946; Glover, 1955) the tendency has nevertheless been to generalize about it from the theories derived from the investigation and treatment of psychotic patients. There are very few clinical studies (as distinguished from theoretical essays) designed to confirm or refute these generalizations or to indicate what, if any, deviations from standard treatment are necessary.

3. RELATIONSHIP OF DEPRESSION TO SCHIZOID AND SCHIZOPHRENIC STATES

One speculative, fascinating but as yet imperfectly understood problem is the relationship between the depressive and the schizoid and schizophrenic states. Kretschmer (1931) attempted to distinguish schizoid and cyclothymic personalities as two fundamental types of contrasting kinds of body structure and temperament.

Fenichel (1945) did not find Kretschmer's attempt at differentiation very helpful, feeling that more important than the differences between these two types was what they had in common, namely a tendency towards narcissistic regression, loss of objects and of reality testing. However, he believed that "the pathogenic fixations of schizophrenia may tentatively be considered as related to a still earlier stage than those found in depressions."

Melanie Klein (1948) and Fairbairn (1952) subscribe to the same thesis which they amplify in considerable detail. Melanie Klein theorized that it was only when the mother could be identified as a whole, real and loved person that the infant could be said to be in the depressive position. It is then that he perceives that the loved object is at the same time the hated object. It is at this time that the infant finds himself confronted with the psychic reality that his hate is directed towards his loved object. The despair and the guilt and the anxiety that this recognition produces go to make up the depressive position.

However, before he experiences the feeling of being loved, i.e., before he can identify the mother as a whole object who loves him, Melanie Klein believes that he is in a phase which is characterized by anxieties about his extreme rage and sadistic fantasies. She postulates that this anxiety is experienced by the infant as a feeling of helplessness and fear in the face of the immense tensions inside himself and of the external persecutors who are the projections of his hate and anger. She believes that a person who has never worked his way through this persecutory-schizoid position and who has never experienced a love relationship in his infancy may all his life have a markedly distorted sense of reality since his persecution-anxiety causes him to see people mainly from the aspect of whether or not they are persecutors. She believes that for such an individual a satisfactory relationship with another object, in the sense of seeing it and understanding it as it really is and loving it, is not possible. And it is this position, she holds, that underlies paranoid and schizophrenic disorders.

Fairbairn differs from Klein in several important theoretical points. He too considers the depressive position as underlying manic-depressive psychosis but his view of this and of the preceding position is considerably different from Klein's. He feels that the child's oral relationship with his mother is his first experience of a social relationship and the foundation upon which he builds all future relationships. According to Fairbairn, a person who is fixated at the late oral phase, after the acquisition of teeth, remains in the depressive position in which his great problem is how to love without destroying by hate. But Fairbairn postulates that in the pre-ambivalent early oral phase when the child relates to his mother

only by sucking, it might appear to the infant who feels that he is
not loved, that the reason for this is that he has destroyed his mother's affection and made it disappear by the very act of his sucking,
i.e., by his first way of expressing love. The intolerable situation
in which he then finds himself is that he perceives his own love as
destructive and bad. The result is that he comes to regard expression of his love as bad, and comes to feel that love relationships in
general are at the very best precarious. Such a person tends to keep
his relationships with his objects in the world of internal reality with
a resulting general over-evaluation of the inner at the expense of the
external world. This is the schizoid position which Fairbairn believes to underlie not only schizophrenia but the very comprehensive schizoid group.

Jacobson (1954), in her metapsychological examination of
psychotic identifications, studies the problem from quite a different
point of view and in the opinion of the writer, from a much more
stimulating one. Her ideas about schizophrenia are, like Melanie
Klein's and Fairbairn's closely related to those about manic-depressive psychosis. About the latter she says that in order to maintain
their self-esteem, manic-depressive patients must at all costs maintain "a continuous libidinous hypercathexis of the love object, designed to prevent its aggressive devaluation in which their self is
bound to participate." Even in psychosis the manic-depressive aims
at and succeeds in remaining dependent on a strong powerful object-
image, the superego. This is presumed to take place, as we have
seen, by means of a regressive transformation of identifications.

Jacobson postulates that in the schizophrenic this regressive process, by virtue of an even more defective ego development, goes
much further. Self- and object-images fuse, not partially as in
manic-depressive psychosis, but much more completely and in a
much more disintegrated manner. In Jacobson's words, "if the
melancholic *treats* himself as if he were the love object, the schizoid
or pre-schizophrenic type imitates, he *behaves* as if he were the object, whereas in a delusional schizophrenic state the patient may
eventually consciously *believe* himself to be another object." Not
only are self and objects confused but the object-representations
may break down into more primitive, infantile, archaic object-
images. "Thus omnipotent, male-female, breast-phallus figures and

castrated, breastless, injured, dead figures" may be created, combining features and traits of various male and female individuals and of the patient himself.

Jacobson refers to the defective ego ideal and superego development in the schizophrenic. His ego ideal is often only an ambitious fantasy of participation in the longed-for omnipotence of the love-objects. In states of psychosis his superego, unlike that of the manic-depressive which gains control of the self, undergoes a regressive transformation back into threatening, murderously primitive parental images. Instead of guilt the patient may experience fears of being persecuted and destroyed or of dying or of being dead.

To sum up, Jacobson also agrees that schizophrenia represents a fixation to an earlier stage of development than manic-depressive psychosis. She however implicitly concurs with Knight (1953) in his suggestion that "a one-sided, libidinal theory of human functioning . . . . needs to be supplemented extensively with the findings of ego psychology." She has therefore offered a theory of psychosis in terms of ego psychology. It is in this ego-psychological sense and with reference to the development of ego and superego identifications that she considers schizophrenia to represent a fixation at and a regression to an earlier developmental phase than manic-depressive psychosis.

Some workers, Cohen and her group for example, feel that manic-depressive psychosis is not only a regressive decompensation to an early stage of personality development, but "can be thought of as serving a defensive function against the still greater personality disintegration which is represented by the schizophrenic state. Thus, in persons whose conflicts and anxiety are too severe to be handled by depressive or manic defenses, a schizophrenic breakdown may be the end result." The implication is that the manic-depressive patient can decompensate even further into a schizophrenic reaction although the authors cite no instances of this in their series.

Jacobson (1954a) fails to provide support for this thesis. She refers to her depressed patients sometimes becoming very confused and sustaining violent psychosomatic reactions while working through deep pre-oedipal material. However she explicitly states that "I have never had the experience of a patient going into a psychotic state provoked by the breaking through of deep id material" except for the recurrence of psychotic depressive episodes. This same issue has occupied the attention of clinical psychiatrists. Lewis and Hubbard (1931), for example, reported on seventy-seven schizophrenic patients at St. Elizabeth's all of whom had originally been diagnosed as manic-depressive. They presumed that they had been erroneously diagnosed on their first admission but the paper did not really conclusively prove that they had not simply become schizophrenic despite correct diagnosis when they were first seen. Similarly Hoch and Rachlin (1941) examined the records of 5799 cases of schizophrenia at the Manhattan State Hospital and found that of this number, 415 cases had been "originally and often repeatedly diagnosed as manic-depressive psychosis." In other words, "every 13th case of schizophrenia was originally diagnosed as manic-depressive psychosis." They felt that most of these cases had had malignant features from the very beginning which had somehow been overlooked. "The description of many cases was often that of schizophrenia, but the diagnosis was manic-depressive, disregarding the basic clinical symptomatology. The diagnosis was probably made because of the quick recovery and periodicity of the attacks, or the presence of so-called psychogenic factors which impressed the examiner so much that he overlooked the fundamental symptoms."

Shortly afterwards Rennie (1942) reported a study of 208 cases of manic-depressive psychosis admitted to the Henry Phipps Psychiatric Clinic and in his review posed the following question: "Does the typical manic-depressive reaction ever change its character sufficiently that one has a right to speak of ultimate schizophrenic development?" He replied that four cases in his series pointed definitely in that direction. There is no implication in his paper that these cases were originally misdiagnosed.

Lewis and Piotrowski (1954) went back to this old problem in an effort to determine whether it was just wisdom after the event that led some psychiatrists to imply that a schizophrenic who had been previously diagnosed manic-depressive had really been schizophrenic all the time or whether there actually were some pathognomonic schizophrenic signs which could guide an experienced observer to the correct diagnosis even in the early deceptive phase of some schizophrenic illnesses. They studied a group of seventy patients originally diagnosed as manic-depressive of whom fifty-four per cent had later developed a clear-cut schizophrenia. They contended that these schizophrenic patients had all had clinical signs—which they classified—at the time of their original diagnosis which should have identified them as schizophrenic even then. They noted "that nearly all errors of diagnosis were made not because of insufficient observation of symptoms but because of failure to interpret the diagnostic significance of the symptoms." They emphasized that "even a trace of schizophrenia is schizophrenia and has a very important prognostic as well as diagnostic significance."

This view is in agreement with that of Bleuler (1911) expressed many years before: "The symptomatological differentiation of schizophrenia from manic-depressive psychosis can only be based on the presence of the specific schizophrenic symptoms. All the phenomena of manic-depressive psychosis may also appear in our disease; the only decisive factor is the presence or absence of schizophrenic symptoms. Therefore, neither a state of manic exaltation nor a melancholic depression, nor the alteration of both states has any significance for the diagnosis. Only after careful observation has revealed no schizophrenic features, may we conclude that we are dealing with a manic-depressive psychosis."

And it must be said that a glance back at the protocols of Rennie's four cases which were alleged to have changed from manic-depressive psychosis to schizophrenia reveals in all of them the presence of symptoms that Lewis and Piotrowski would claim were pathognomonic of schizophrenia, e.g. (1) (The patient) felt people were taking advantage of her, heard voices, smelled disagreeable odors .... and .. had ideas of persecution and influence;" (2) "(she) could feel that Satan was going around in her head;" (3) "an agitated depression with catatonic features;" (4) "She immediately became fearful, suspicious, agitated, sleepless, thought people were plotting against her, that she was spied on by her neighbors, that she was accused of stealing. She had auditory hallucinations of a depressive character."

In support of the above observations one might also cite Kallman's (1953) observation that schizophrenia and manic-depressive psychosis do not occur in the same family unit if the diagnostic criteria for these conditions are properly restricted.

4. SEMANTICS OF "DEPRESSION"

Attention should here be drawn to a paradoxical situation, namely that although the numerous writers discussed in this review have all written copiously about depression there is nevertheless no widespread agreement in the literature as to what the phenomenon of depression actually comprises.

Whitehorn (1939) has commented on the naivete of uncritically believing that one can easily label a patient's "emotions" by listening to the conventional terms which he uses to describe them. It would seem that nowhere is this danger more threatening than when the patient states that he is depressed.

The difference between two depressive syndromes have impressed one observer so markedly that he argues that although these disparate clinical pictures are both designated "depression" one of them is in reality something quite different. Fairbairn, according to Guntrip (1952), feels that "complaints of feeling cut off, shut off, out of touch, feeling apart or strange, of things being out of focus or unreal, of not feeling well with people, interest flagging, things seeming futile and meaningless" all describe a state of mind which patients often call "depression" but which "lacks the heavy, black, inner sense of brooding, of anger and of guilt, which are not difficult to discover in depression." Fairbairn refers to the states of mind describing above as "schizoid states."

Similarly, Good (1946) divides depressions into two groups. The first group consists of those conditions ordinarily classified as the depressed phase of manic-depressive psychosis. The patient belonging to this group has lost touch with reality, is retarded, complains in a low monotonous voice of having committed grave and unforgivable sins, of being eternally damned and destined to endure the tortures of hell. He reproaches and vilifies himself and may refuse food or may demand that he be done away with.

A typical patient in the second group retains the ability to smile and to communicate and may appear deceptively normal. He may describe his complaints in various ways: " 'I don't get the same kick out of things as I used to,' 'I feel as if I had a big disappointment only it lasts,' 'things don't seem worth while,' 'fed up,' 'browned off,' 'as if the joy had gone out of life,' of the color having faded from life, from the things which constitute life, of life being insipid, tasteless, full, and monotonous; 'things don't matter' or 'I don't give a damn—nothing left to bother about—not worth carrying on for,' etc. Seldom do self-reproaches accompany the verbal expression of these feelings." Good refers to this second type of depression as "schizophrenic depression" in contrast to the first type which he designates as "melancholic."

By 1951 we find that Rado had lost his earlier (1928) more simple view of depression sufficiently to remark: "We encounter depressions in drug-dependent patients, neurotics, schizophrenics, general paretics, patients afflicted with severe physical illness, etc. The question arises whether or not significant psychodynamic differences exist between depressive spells that occur in different pathogenic contexts. Further psychoanalytic investigation may provide an answer to this question."

Indeed it was a very pertinent question. Whether the formulations chiefly derived from the study of a small group of manic-depressive patients are as applicable to the restlessly agitated depressive psychoses of the involutional period, the empty, lonely depressed conditions found in young schizophrenics and the listless apathetic post-viral depressions as they are to the deeply retarded periodic melancholias of the manic-depressive type is a very pertinent inquiry. It is one which workers had tended to ignore or to answer with misplaced and unwarranted confidence.

Gero (1953) addressed himself to this same question. He uttered a warning about the dangers inherent in not clearly recognizing the nature of the clinical material forming the basis of any particular theory. He pointed out that "we do not always realize that we are talking about different phenomena and arrive at theories which contradict each other." He not only believed that all depressed patients do not necessarily belong to the same clinical groups which Freud and Abraham studied, but he also felt that even "in the same type of depression different aspects of the symptomatology necessitate different explanations."

It is noteworthy that Engel and Reichsman (1956) in their extraordinarily interesting study of the infant Monica conclude that their observations lead them "to the position that there is not only the active, oral, introjective anlage emphasized in classic theory" (characterized by "the varieties of internalization of aggression") but "also an active, pre-oral, pre-object anlage" which is psychologically . . . . well expressed by Bibring's (1953) phrase, 'the ego's shocking awareness of its helplessness in regard to its aspirations.' " These conclusions appear to bear striking kinship to those of Fairbairn and of Good although expressed in different terms and derived from different patient material.

Stunkard (1957) too is impressed with how little the classical psychodynamic formulations of depression are applicable to the depressed obese patients whom he has been studying. He describes these patients as follows: "The predominant symptomatology was depressive, but they were not typical depressions. The closest parallel is perhaps those curious periods of apathy and sadness which occur during the adolescence of schizoid people." He particularly notes the absence of expressions of self-condemnation.

5. "DEPRESSIVE EQUIVALENTS"

In a series of papers, Kaufman (1955; 1956 with Elizabeth Makkay: 1958; 1958 with Lora Heims) elaborates his concept that delinquency is frequently the juvenile delinquent's method of coping with his underlying depression or his "depressive nucleus" as Kaufman refers to it. He sees the child's delinquency as partly an attempt to avoid confronting and experiencing his overwhelming depression. He sees it in other words, as a sort of equivalent of depression or, more precisely, as a defense against depression.

The term "manic-depressive equivalent," was actually coined in 1944 by Foster Kennedy to designate somatic complaints following a periodic course in the absence of or with mood changes. Long before this it was clearly understood that depressed patients, manic-depressive or otherwise, often complained of somatic sensations in addition to or as a substitute for their depressed mood. Every psychiatrist has seen such patients admitted to one medical ward after another for the fruitless investigation of constipation or gastric distress. And countless patients have been subjected to surgery because of the failure to recognize the depressive nature of the somatic complaint. Many psychiatrists (e.g., Jones, 1949) writing in the general medical literature have warned of the dangers of overlooking such "depressive equivalents."

Lorand (1946) and Gero (1953) have contributed to the elucidation of one particular equivalent of depression, anorexia. It is unnecessary to dwell upon the details of this except to note with Gero the difficulty in explaining any particular choice of symptom. He points out that "the nature of the oral drive pattern does not determine the symptom. Not all depressive patients with the same cannibalistic or oral-sadistic drives, with the same incorporative needs, develop eating disturbances. A complicated set of factors, not all of them necessarily recognizable, will decide whether or not an eating disturbance results."

The term "depressive equivalent" carries the connotation that the particular symptom complained of exists without the corresponding mood accompaniment. A patient for example may complain of constipation without being aware of its affective significance, without clearly knowing that he is depressed. But whether the patient is or is not conscious of his depression, this type of somatic complaint represents in general a change in function or body sensation rather than a detectable tissue alteration. When a depressed and constipated patient for example is investigated by x-ray or sigmoidoscope no tissue pathology is visible.

There are cases however where the depressed mood does seem to exist in some significant relationship to a pathological process in the body tissues. Although he does not stress the accompanying affect, Alxander (1950) cites many instances of psychosomatic disorders occurring after object loss when one might ordinarily expect depressed feelings to manifest themselves. More specifically McClary, Meyer and Weitzman (1955) have observed a very suggestive relationship between depression and disseminated lupus erythematosis in a series of fourteen patients. These patients appeared to have a characteristic series of reactions to the loss or the threat of loss of a significant person. These situations were at first reacted to with denial, especially denial of the intensity of the emotional experience. This denial would be followed by a tense need for increased activity and when this did not suffice or could not be maintained, depression and pain and joint disability appeared.

And Engel (1955) in his study of ulcerative colitis considers it "an arresting observation" that the feeling tone at the time of onset or relapse of symptoms in every instance in which he could obtain the appropriate data in his series of 39 patients (there were 45 such instances) "was designated by such expressions as 'helpless,' 'despair,' 'hopeless,' 'overwhelmed,' 'too much to cope with,' 'too much to expect of me.' " "In general," he goes on to say, "there was a fairly good correlation between the severity of the symptoms and the degree of helplessness or hopelessness felt by the patient."

Incidentally, his case material as well as that of several other writers quoted by him contain instances of colitis co-existing with psychotic depression. These observations do not provide support, as Engel points out, for an impression frequently encountered in the literature that psychoses and psychosomatic disorders have a reciprocal relationship.

In a study of 42 semiprivate hospitalized medical patients Schmale (1958) reports on the relationship that he has observed between separation and depression on the one hand and disease on the other. He refers to "separation and depression" as "the psychic pattern of unsuccessful resolution of object loss." In 41 of the 42 patients in his series the author felt "that there was verbal and/or nonverbal evidence for feelings of helplessness or hopelessness prior to the onset of the disease." This investigator sees disease as "one possible manifestation of depression" but acknowledges that it is by no means understood why these patients responded to separation with medical illness rather than just with depression.

Engel (1954) too calls attention to the importance of determining how the psychological processes in ulcerative colitis are related to the somatic (and of course the same holds true for every similar disorder): "The jump from the psychic phenomena to the physical phenomena at the end organ is conceptually the most difficult . . . " Engel has heeded his own summons to study the physiology of hope and despair and has recently (1955a) reported an extensive and rigorous investigation of the effect of mood on gastric physiology.

However, an understanding of the biochemical changes that take place even in depressions not complicated by overt psychosomatic disturbances is still rudimentary. The literature is of course replete with studies and surveys of this aspect of depression. But Sperry (1954) has concluded "that there is no consistent deviation from normal in the concentration of any of the constituents of the blood which have been extensively studied in depressed patients, with the possible exception of cholesterol." Nevertheless he feels that it has been reasonably established that the concentrations of blood constituents in depressed patients are more variable than in normal subjects. In other words, "biochemical homeostasis is under less rigid control in the former than in the latter."

Chapter VI

TREATMENT

Despite the original psychoanalytic pessimism about the treatment of the so-called "narcissistic neuroses" one finds in the early literature a recurring cautious advocacy of analysis for patients with manic-depressive psychosis. Abraham (1911) perhaps set the tone with his rather determined optimism. He declared that psychoanalysis was "the only rational therapy to apply to the manic-depressive psychosis." Of the six patients in his series two had already completed their analyses. One of these analyses had taken what seems now to have been the unusually short period of six months. Abraham acknowledged that "it is usually extraordinarily difficult to establish a transference in these patients who have turned away from all the world in their depression" and he advised that treatment should be begun during the free intervals between their attacks because he did not feel that analysis could be carried on with severely inhibited depressed patients.

Other papers on the analyses of manic-depressives began to appear as early as 1914. In that year Clark reported the successful treatment of two cases of "periodic mental depression." Contrary to the views generally held at that time on the treatment of such patients, Clark observed "that the transference occurs rapidly and is extraordinarily strong." In a later communication (1919) he considered, like Abraham, that severe depressives were not analyzable, but by 1923 he was able to add ten more successful cases to his series. All of these patients had had serious depressive illnesses and none of them had relapsed up to the time of his report. He felt that the periods when the patient was entering into or emerging from a depression were the most propitious times to start treatment.

Barkas (1925) also disagreed with current analytic opinion on the subject of the transference in the treatment of psychotic patients: "It has been said that the fundamental difficulty in the treatment of the psychoses lies in the difficulty of establishing a transference relationship; no one who has worked in a mental hospital can uphold this statement. Transference, both positive and negative, occurs violently towards the persons of the environment and is used intuitively by the staff of any asylum, and patients of all types respond to some extent."

By 1924, Abraham had come to feel that, in addition to relieving symptoms, the treatment of the manic-depressive should safeguard the patient from further attacks of illness. Ideally the treatment should do away with his regressive libidinal impulses and should "effect a progression of his libido until he reaches the stage of genital organization and complete object-love." Abraham was able to report that one of his patients had become able to enter into normal object-relationships and had ceased to regard himself as a monstrosity, which he had previously done even in his free periods. Two of his patients, in situations where they would previously have withdrawn into melancholia, had developed instead transitory phobic, obsessional or hysteric symptoms. Abraham regarded it as highly noteworthy that these patients had ascended from a melancholic to a hysteric level.

There followed in the next decade or so a series of reports (e.g., Feigenbaum, 1926; Peck, 1939) which confirmed many of the observations of Abraham, Freud and Rado with regard to treatment. As was characteristic of that period in the history of psychoanalysis the main focus of treatment was on the patient's id. Treatment consisted mainly of making the unconscious conscious, i.e., of making the patient aware of his repressed impulses.

However in 1933 Reich called attention to one type of resistance to analytic treatment which he labelled "character resistance." By this term he meant a kind of resistance which was deeply imbedded in the personality structure of the patient and which was indeed characteristic of that patient. There were presumed to be as many types of character resistance as there were types of character structure. This resistance could for example take the form of compliance or rigidity or aggressiveness. Reich felt that an analysis could not be carried on successfully until these resistances had been exposed and rendered inoperative. He described the analysis of character resistance as taking place systematically through the layers of its historical development, a process which he termed "character analysis."

Under the influence of Reich's work, Gero in 1936 made the next major contribution to the treatment of depression. He considered that the depressive's infantile demands for love remain unfulfilled because the normal adult method of gratifying these infantile wishes for warmth and tenderness, namely the genital love-relationship, remains barred to these patients. He felt that this method of experiencing and acquiring love remains closed to them because of the anxieties and guilt associated with this libidinal phase. He felt that these patients therefore "long for something unattainable, being grown up, they want to be loved like children." Gero considered that the fundamental analytic task in their treatment was the mastery of the genital anxieties which "press the libido back into the pregenital positions" and which cause the patients to long for immoderate infantile satisfactions which they cannot obtain.

In the treatment of such patients, Gero stressed the importance of character analysis, i.e., the discovery and loosening of the specific characterological defenses that these patients employ. After these defenses against the underlying intense infantile cravings have become weakened the patient becomes aware of and experiences his deeply repressed oral wishes. Gero emphasized that it was not enough for the analyst to call attention to these unconscious wishes. He must bring it about that the patient actually experiences these cravings, an experience that is always, according to Gero, "accompanied by the appearance of bodily sensations, by violent affects and by great anxiety."

The solution of the oral fixation now becomes possible. Gero observed that "experiencing the oral wishes means at the same time becoming conscious of the object towards which these wishes are directed. . . . . The solution of the oral fixation is attained less by the adult neurotic becoming conscious of his infantile wishes, and being thus able to resign these wishes which he now recognizes as infantile, than by his consciousness that he desires the breast—that is to say—the mother; and having become aware of this, the infantile wish to nestle close to the mother, the longing for the warm caressing body of the mother arouse also those dark and ardent wishes of a later time of childhood when he fell passionately in love with his mother. Consciousness of oral wishes turns into genital excitement. That is why the actual experiencing of oral wishes in analysis brings with it genital sensations. The solution of the oral fixations is therefore attained if one succeeds in making the patient experience the repressed oral impulses, for this experience does not stop at the oral aims, but activates the genital object-relation of the Oedipus-situation."

The next important technical problem in the analysis of depressives, according to Gero, is the bringing of the aggression into consciousness. It is again not sufficient simply to interpret the aggression. It is necessary to loosen the patient's defenses so that he can consciously experience his rage and hostility in the transference situation. It is finally necessary for this aggression to be worked out through its many layers and fixation points until the "aggressive impulses originating from the central conflict of the Oedipus situation" are made conscious and the genital anxieties and guilt mastered so that "the capacity of experiencing genital life and object-relations to the full, and without ambivalence is re-established."

In 1945 Fenichel summarized the current views on the therapeutic analysis of manic-depressive conditions. He cited three special types of difficulties which must be overcome in the treatment of these patients. The first was the oral fixation, "the remoteness of crucial infantile experiences which the analysis must uncover." The second was the looseness and ambivalence of the transference. And the third was the inaccessibility of the severely depressed patient. He therefore, like Abraham (1924), recommended the free interval as the period of choice for treatment but drew attention to the observation which had also been made by Abraham and other workers that even inaccessible patients who do not appear to be in contact with the world are grateful and may sometimes derive benefit from a patient listener. Fenichel's tempered optimism about the treatment of manic-depressives is revealed in his remark that "even if the analysis fails, the patient is temporarily relieved through the opportunity of unburdening himself by talking." He was much more sanguine about the treatment of neurotic depressives. He felt that they needed no special techniques and presented no problems not found in other neurotic conditions.

Somewhat at variance with this view is Lorand's (1946) report of his experience with a case of neurotic depression in which he had found it necessary to deviate considerably from standard analytic technique, at least in the early states of treatment. For example he had found it advisable to prescribe medications and to change appointments "according to (the patient's) inconsequential personal program." He had moreover at first made considerable use of encouragement and guidance.

To come back to the subject of psychotic depressions, Lampl-de Groot (1953) also feels that a deeply melancholic patient is not amenable to analytic therapy. In her paper she reviews the factors that she considers of importance in determining success or failure in the therapy of depression. In her opinon, the presence of sadomasochistic urges or fantasies militates against success. "An intimate fusion of (aggressive drives) with libido" worsens the prognosis whereas aggressive urges which are not fused with the libidinal drive "can be liberated from repression and eventually integrated into the personality."

She considers the patient's capacity for sublimating his aggression to be a measure of his ability to improve. Taking a position similar to that of Hartmann, Kris and Loewenstein (1949) she feels that aggression, like the libidinal drive, can be sublimated in pursuits like exploration, the acquisition of knowledge, the control of nature, surgery, engineering, etc.

Finally she believes that the form of discharge of aggression predominantly present in a patient is of importance in prognosis. According to her, aggression can be discharged directly as destructive or aggressive acts or outbursts of rage, or more indirectly by " 'gaining possession of,' conquering, mastering, getting hold of an object" in which the object is not destroyed but rather serves to increase the subject's power. She feels that when the patient's aggression is discharged in the latter way, by gaining possession of the object, his prognosis is better than when his aggression is discharged via "the mode of destruction," particularly when his sublimatory capacities are limited.

Mabel Blake Cohen and her colleagues (1954) and Edith Jacobson (1954) have recently reported on their experience with the psychoanalytic treatment of manic-depressive patients. They consider this topic largely from the point of view of transference and countertransference phenomena. Cohen *et al.* feel that these patients have two outstanding transference patterns. The first of these patterns is their coercive manipulative dependency. Manic-depressive patients demand gratification by a verbalized and unverbalized exploitative demonstration of their own misery and need and of the other person's selfish indifference and culpability if he does not respond to this need.

The second of these patterns is their striking insensitivity to the individual characteristics of other people. They respond to others in a stereotyped way which clearly indicates that they simply do not see them as individuals in their own right. Like Melanie Klein (1948), Cohen and her colleagues believe that the manic-depressive is fixated at that depressive position where the mother has just begun to be recognized as a whole person, i.e., when it is discovered that the former "bad mother" and the former "good mother" are in reality the same individual. There are many anxieties associated with this position. The child experiences gratifying feelings of fulfillment and "goodness" when the mother is "good." But when she is rejecting or frustrating or in other words a "bad mother" this "makes the child hateful, enraged, bad, and fills him with bad emotional content that he tries to get rid of by elimination or denial." Melanie Klein believes that the manic-depressive has never successfully worked through this position, i.e., his early good experiences have not been sufficient to permit him to overcome his depressive anxiety when his mother is "bad." He has, in other words, not learned how to maintain his self-esteem through this period of maternal "badness". He is therefore continuously engaged in an operation of transforming the bad mother into a good one, and of denying her "badness." It is this that constitutes his interpersonal sterotypy.

The lack of interpersonal sensitivity which these patients display in their dealings with people is of course clearly observable in their relations with the therapist who is regarded "(a) as an object to be manipulated for purposes of getting sympathy and reassurance, (b) as a moral authority who can be manipulated into giving approval, and (c) as, in actuality, a critical and rejecting authority figure who will not give real approval but can be counted on only for token approval which can be achieved by proper behavior or manipulation."

The authors at first tended to regard this interpersonal obtuseness as a real learning defect in their patients but gradually came to understand it as actually a defense against the anxiety of having to recognize the simultaneous presence of good and bad traits in the same person. These patients have not yet come to terms with the anxiety of acknowledging the presence of "bad" traits in "good" objects. The recognition of unacceptable components in the other person would entail the abandonment of such an individual by the manic-depressive. In order to defend himself against this anxiety the manic-depressive avoids the recognition of this complexity of personality structure, of the mixture of "good" and "bad" traits in every person and thus deprives himself of the possibility of entertaining a wide spectrum of complex feelings.

The writers give serious consideration to the technical problems of dealing with these two transference patterns. They discuss the danger of the unmodified classical technique with its relatively passive therapeutic role which seems to mean to these patients a promise that their dependency needs will some day be met and that the therapist will eventually be manipulated into the parent role which they want him to play. Sooner or later the patient will interpret something in the therapist's behavior as a rejection, and, having to give up his gratification fantasies, he will become hopeless and suicidal. The same result may occur if the therapist is openly rejecting of the patient's demands. At first there will be a redoubling of efforts to please the harsh authority figure and to extort signs of approval, but, this failing too, hopelessness and perhaps a suicidal attempt will follow.

One of the counter-transference difficulties reported by Cohen and her group is precisely in the area of the patient's demandingness. Some therapists, particularly those prone to play benign roles with patients, may find that these patients are actually succeeding in manipulating them. The recognition of this fact may bring about a sudden resentment and perhaps rejection of the patient. It was discovered that even therapists who seemed to have no trouble dealing with the demandingness of these patients actually manifested a certain degree of apprehension of which they were unaware.

Another countertransference problem that was noted was that analysts who work with psychotics prefer to treat schizoid and schizophrenic patients. The extraverted, interpersonally stereotyped manic-depressive seems shallow, superficial, insensitive and unresponsive to such analysts, who, themselves, tend to be obsessional or schizoid people.* It was the impression of the group that cyclothymic therapists actually do better with such patients. However it was noted that the interest of all of the workers in the project increased considerably when some conceptions of how to deal with these patients came into being. It was agreed by all the members of the group that the first step in therapy was to get beyond the interpersonal stereotypy and conventionalized barrier of these patients and into the area of meaningful emotional exchange. In other words the first step was to come to grips with the characterological defenses of these patients. Various therapeutic maneuvers were proposed and utilized for this purpose: nonverbal techniques, a more patient intense application of the usual techniques, pressing the patient for material that was presumed to be present and available, occasional outbursts by the therapist, etc.

The latter event occurred a few times and with one patient the spontaneously expressed anger succeeded in putting a halt to the stereotyped complaining and allowed an exchange of feeling to occur. The fact that the therapist was human enough to get angry seemed to make the episode significant for the patient. However the authors caution that "it is, of course, highly speculative whether such a sudden, spontaneous eruption of the therapist could be fashioned into a planned technical approach."

The research group found itself in agreement about the matter of

*For example, Clark in 1923 stated: "While it may sound unsympathetic, and also the facts may have been drawn from too few data, yet intense preoccupation with the manic-depressive group as a whole gives the impression that such individuals do not take a deep-rooted grasp upon the foundations of life, and though usually pleasing in personality have no great staying qualities. Just as the epileptic has many of these stabilizing qualities even to excess, the depressant is more superficial and possesses too little tough fiber for life's stress and storm."

handling the patient's demands. There was a consensus that this was a problem involving dangerous risks but that it was safest and most therapeutic for the irrational demands to be recognized, brought out into the open, labelled, discussed with the patient and refused. Furthermore it was also agreed that the patient's manipulation of the therapist by acting out in the form of failure either at work or in the life situation or by threats of suicide should be handled by "a denial of responsibility for the continued existence of the patient," coupled with an implication or admission that the patient was important or meaningful to the therapist. The patient may feel that the therapist cannot be interested in him unless he needs him, e.g., unless he needs to succeed therapeutically with the patient for the sake of his own reputation. The writers suggest that the patient be made to understand that the therapist can be interested in the patient as a person without at the same time being dependent upon him for his reputation. They also recommend that the therapist should continuously attempt to convey his own feelings and attitudes to the patient so that the latter can gain some sense of his own meaningfulness to the therapist.

In short, these workers stressed the importance of the demandingness and the emotional stereotypy in the transference patterns of these patients. They also described their experiences with countertransference problems and with techniques for establishing meaningful communication with these patients and for handling their dependency needs. They acknowledged the desirability of further study in these areas.

These writers worked largely in the conceptual framework of Sullivan's interpersonal theory although they did not hesitate to take advantage of the contributions of the more orthodox analytic workers and, as a matter of fact, acknowledged a particular debt to the theories of Melanie Klein. Their work, as reported, is notable for its exclusive concern with patterns of interpersonal relationships and for its neglect of the usual pregenital fantasy material that was reported so copiously by previous writers.

However, Jacobson (1954b) too, despite her different theoretical orientation explicitly states that in some depressed patients it is simply not possible "to carry the analysis of such patients to the point where their preoedipal fantasies and impulses are produced and interpreted" although her experience suggests "that the more thorough and lasting therapeutic results could be achieved in cases where this deep fantasy material could be fully revived, understood and digested."

The central theme of her paper also concerns the problems arising from the demandingness of these patients. She discusses the technical difficulties associated with the fact that they inevitably make the analyst their central love object and the focus of their pathological demands. It is interesting that Jacobson and Cohen and her colleagues have recognized similar problems and dangers and, in many cases, have advocated similar technical procedures in the treatment of these patients.

Jacobson, like Cohen and her co-authors, emphasizes the danger of seeming to offer these patients "seductive promises too great to be fulfilled." To avoid this, she advises that early in the analysis, in connection with interpretations regarding the illusory nature of the patients' expectations, that one should utter warnings about the future. She too advocates deviations from the classical technique. For example, she advises only three or four sessions per week, because she believes that this tends to reduce rather than increase the ambivalence of these patients. She has noted that daily sessions are interpreted by them either as unspoken and really unfulfillable promises or as intolerable obligations which must be masochistically submitted to.

However, in accordance with her recommendation for a flexible application of analytic technique, she acknowledges that more frequent or longer sessions may sometimes be necessary with very deeply depressed patients. And she notes that during such periods the analyst may serve merely as a patient listener providing the patient "maybe for weeks or months not more than support from a durable transference, which may carry them through the depression."

One of the analyst's difficult tasks is to adjust his responses and remarks to the patient's psychological rhythm. This is essentially an exercise in subtle empathy. "There must be a continuous, subtle, empathic tie between the analyst and his depressive patients; we must be very careful not to let empty silences grow or not to talk too long, too rapidly and too emphatically; that is, never to give too much or too little . . . . What those patients need is a . . . . sufficient amount of spontaneity and flexible adjustment to their mood level, of warm understanding and especially of unwavering respect; attitudes which must not be confused with overkindness, sympathy, reassurance, etc. In periods of threatening narcissistic withdrawal we may have to show a very active interest and participation in their daily activities and especially their sublimations." Like Cohen *et al.,* Jacobson remarks that analysts who tend to be detached in temperament seem to have greater difficulty in treating these patients.

Interestingly enough, Jacobson too takes up the matter of the apparently almost inevitable occasional spontaneous flash of anger on the part of the therapist. She believes that this is a most precarious event since it too in a sense is a response to the patient's demandingness, for not only does he demand love and affection but at times he unconsciously demands a show of power from the analyst. As she observed in an earlier paper (1953), when the patient finds that the analyst is no longer able to live up to his expectations of love, he may, in his fear of a complete loss of his object, regress a step further. "The patient may now attempt to hold on at least to the reanimated image of an omnipotent, not loving, but primitive sadistic object." He may try to bring down upon himself a show of strictness, anger and punishment. Thus Jacobson adds an additional dimension to the explanation given by Cohen *et al.,* for the occasionally therapeutic result of an outburst of anger by the therapist. They felt that it demonstrated to the patient that the analyst was human and that he cared. Jacobson adds in effect, that the patient prefers an angry therapist to a nonparticipating one, a punitive object to no object. This explosion of anger sometimes serves to carry the patient over a dangerous depressive stage, but in view of the provocativeness of these patients, she advocates "the most careful self-scrutiny and self-control in the analyst."

Jacobson places great emphasis on the vicissitudes of the transference in these patients. The problem is, as she sees it, to let the intensely ambivalent transference of these patients develop sufficiently for analysis to take place without the patient eventually discontinuing analysis in a phase of spurious transference success or, on the other hand, in a phase of severe depression. To emphasize these difficulties, to which she confesses she can offer no completely satisfactory solution, she outlines typical phases in the analyses of these patients.

The first phase may be marked by the establishment of prompt, intense rapport with the analyst, reflected in idealized fantasies about him and in marked enthusiasm for the treatment. Improvement may follow rapidly. But it is a deceptive improvement which depends on the unrealistic magical quality of the transference feelings and on the "exaggerated idealization and obstinate denial of possible or visible shortcomings of the analyst," distortions not dissimilar to those described by Cohen and her group. No real change occurs in the patient but his mood is one of hope and optimism. A successful analysis seems certain to him, although perhaps not until a long time in the future.

This phase may then be followed by a period of growing disappointment which is marked by sporadic doubts about the excellence, wisdom and kindness of the analyst followed by immediate efforts to transform him again into the loving, idealized image of his former fantasies. Feelings of hopelessness and self-doubt increase. Manifestations of ambivalence become more marked and may be displaced for a time to a third person, perhaps the spouse. A long typical period may follow in which the patient becomes more and more involved in the analysis and withdraws dangerously from other interpersonal relationships. Dependent, masochistic attitudes now characterize the transference, accompanied by demands for self-sacrificing devotion. The transference becomes more ambivalent and the patient, with his attempts to arouse guilt in the analyst for his alleged mistreatment of him, becomes more exhaustingly provocative.

Such a phase may be followed by a deepening of the depression in which the patient may totally abandon the "bad" object and enter a stage of pathological introjective defenses and narcissistic withdrawal, i.e., his restitutive maneuvers may now be enacted entirely in the psychic plane. The danger of discontinuation of therapy in this phase is great.

However, despite the unanswered questions that she freely raises, Jacobson is able to report some considerable success with these trying and difficult patients. She emphasizes the importance of a slow and careful analysis of their transference conflicts, their ego distortions and their superego defects which would seem to be essentially equivalent to what Cohen and her group refer to as their demandingness, their provocativeness, their interpersonal insensitivity and their distortion of every person into approving or disapproving parental figures.

It is interesting that many topics which so exclusively preoccupied previous writers on depression—such as the depressive's self-reproaches, his hostile introjection of the abandoned object, the freeing of his hostility in treatment—now, in the broader perspective of the recent workers, find their place as mere phases in the interpersonal and transference conflicts of these very difficult patients.

Chapter VII

CONCLUSIONS

1.

IT WOULD HAVE BEEN PLEASING to be able to report that this body of literature represented, in essence, a progress through the years of a Great Investigation. It does so in part. But perhaps even more does it represent a Great Debate with the rhetorical rather than scientific implications of this word. Indeed at times it bears the stigmata not of an exchange of ideas but of a Monologue—a Not-So-Great Monologue.

To one familar with the open confessions of ignorance in other scientific disciplines it is a little disconcerting to read the confidently proffered global conclusions of the literature on depression. This tendency to erect comprehensive theoretical systems makes it seem as if legitimate uncertainty has acquired the bar sinister.

According to Whitehorn (1955), "It could be said with some justification that the scientist's first duty is to doubt." And perhaps high in priority among those things which a sophisticated worker should doubt is the absolute validity of his own formulations. Konrad Lorenz (1955) has said that he takes pains to make himself as stupid as possible and to misunderstand everything that he could possibly misunderstand. By contrast the literature on depression exhibits a recurrent tendency to gloss over disagreement with previous writers.

There exists an impression that psychoanalytical writing is still polemical. In fact, contemporary analytic writers appear almost reluctant to engage in open controversy. Despite this reluctance, however, there is but limited consensus among writers on depression. Disagreement is acute on numerous issues: for example, the period in childhood which is most critical for the predisposition to depression, the frequency of orality in depressed states and its significance when present, and the relationship of aggressive drives to depression.

One factor detracting from the scientific workmanship of the literature on depression is the frequently inadequate delineation of the case material. A sine qua non of scientific presentation is the description of the clinical group under discussion. Abraham and Freud were careful to identify diagnostically the depressed patients they were discussing. On one occasion, in order to corroborate the diagnosis of two of his patients, Abraham (1924) went so far as to report that they had "repeatedly been put in asylums or sanatoriums where they were under the observation of able psychiatrists and . . . . (that) they had been examined by eminent mental specialists. The clinical picture was absolutely typical (of manic-depressive psychosis) and the circular course of the illness quite characteristic in both cases."

In contrast with such careful reporting, many theories are based on case material that is described no more precisely than by the word "depressed." Emotional disorders are not clearly identified and the size of the sample is rarely mentioned. Instead, the theoretical conclusions are announced ex cathedra, as it were, based on the writer's presumably extensive experience.

One could be appreciative of any particular worker's range of experience and still wish more precise knowledge about his sample of patients. Kubie (1952), for example, notes that "even in the course of a lifetime of exclusive devotion to the psychoanalytic treatment of patients no analyst will have been able to analyze deeply more than a few representatives of any one psychopathological constellation." Mabel Blake Cohen and three colleagues studied a group of manic-depressive patients over a period of several years and were able to report on a series no larger than twelve cases.

Another failing in the literature on depression is the assumption that features noted in one's own patients must necessarily be found in all similar patients. Gero (1936), for example, in his report on two patients assumed that their failure to achieve genital relationships was characteristic of all depressed patients. Yet Jacobson (1953) in her description of manic-depressives notes that "in their sexual life they may show a full genital response."

2.

There is now ample evidence that the term "depression" covers a variety of affective states which differ not only overtly, but also subjectively. Many of the previous formulations of depression and of the depressive character structure are simply not comprehensive enough to do justice to the variety of clinical types. Depressed patients are to be found not only among those who are excessively dependent for self-esteem on external narcissistic supplies; nor on the other hand are depressed patients to be found only among rigid over-conscientious perfectionists who expect the impossible of themselves. The spectrum is not nearly so narrow.

This relative multiplicity of depressed states—associated in some instances perhaps with private biases on the parts of the authors—has led to a variety of psychodynamic formulations and conceptualizations of the depressive reactions, each with partial validity but with only too many of them implicitly claiming general application. For different writers "depression" has not only different components but also different purposes. For one author, it is, in essence emptiness and loneliness; for another it is rage and guilt. For one observer it is a passive consequence of having sustained a loss in self-esteem; for another, it is an active though distorted attempt to undo this losss.

A more widespread awareness of the complexity and the variety of the depressive reactions will perhaps give rise to less dogmatic and more sophisticated theoretical models.

A striking feature of the impressionistic word pictures of depression painted by many writers is that they have the flavor of art rather than of science and may well represent profound personal intuitions as much as they depict the raw clinical data.

For Abraham for example, the depressed state appears to have been a complicated process of psychic digestion shot through with primitive desires and impulses and fantasies. Freud saw melancholia as a loud lamenting self-tormenting period of mourning in which each and every tie with the introjected love object is painfully loosened and abandoned. Melanie Klein and Fairbairn view depression as a mixture of sorrow over the loss of the love object and of guilt over the hostility and rage that brought about this loss. Balint by way of contrast thinks of depression as essentially a state of starved unhappy lovelessness not necessarily reactive to previous sadistic fantasies. For Fairbairn such a condition in which hostility and guilt are absent is not depression at all but merits a special term the "schizoid state."

Rado pictured a depression as a great despairing cry for love and forgiveness, a drama of expiation acted out on the psychic plane following upon a fall in self-esteem. Fenichel, too, conceptualized depression as being simultaneously a fall in self-esteem and an attempt to coerce the love-object into delivering the narcissistic supplies necessary to restore the self-esteem. He and Rado both felt that this formulation was broad enough to apply to all cases of depression.

Both Bibring and Jacobson felt that there was a mechanism common to all cases of depression but differed from Rado and Fenichel in their conception of it. Bibring saw the fall in self-esteem as the essential element in depression with all else—including the restitutive attempts when they occur—as secondary phenomena. Jacobson, on the other hand, ascribed "the central part in the pathology of depression to aggression and its vicissitudes."

From each personal vision of depression stem derivative explanations of one or another depressive symptom. The guilt of which the depressive complains, for example, was viewed by Abraham in conformity with his particular picture of this condition as related to the patient's cannibalistic impulses. Rado, with his conception of depression as a prolonged attempt to win back the love object understood the patient to be guilty because by his aggressive attitude he has himself to blame for the loss of the object. Mabel Blake Cohen and her group think of the patient's guilt as essentially a device to manipulate the object and to win approval. As they put it, "the patient merely resorts to the magic of uttering cries to placate authority."

3.

Those writers who have concerned themselves with the importance of loss of self-esteem in depression have conceptualized the circumstances and the nature of this loss in somewhat different terms. Rado, for example, thought that self-esteem was essentially dependent on external narcissistic supplies, at least in persons prone to depression. Depressive patients "have a sense of security and comfort only when they feel themselves loved, esteemed, supported and encouraged . . . . They are like those children, who when their early narcissism is shattered, recover their self-respect only in complete dependence on their love objects."

Fenichel, on the other hand, while agreeing that depressions occur in persons who are fixated at the point where their self-esteem is regulated by external supplies, appeared to have a broader conception of the events that cause a fall in self-esteem in depressives. In addition to the loss of love, whether by disappointment or by the death of the love partner, he listed a variety of possible precipitating circumstances. These included "experiences, which, for a normal person would also imply loss of self-esteem, such as failures, loss of prestige, loss of money, a state of remorse . . . . or tasks which the patient has to fulfill and which, objectively or subjectively, make him more aware of his 'inferiority' and narcissistic needs; paradoxically, even experiences that for a normal person would mean an increase in self-esteem may precipitate a depression if the success frightens the patient as a threat of punishment or retaliation, or as an imposition for further tasks, thus augmenting his need for supplies."

Since Bibring and Jacobson agree that loss of self-esteem is basic to all types of depression and that a lowered self-esteem may have many different causes, they necessarily feel that depressed states may arise from a multitude of sources. Bibring felt that the loss of self-esteem in depression results from the tension between highly important aspirations and an awareness of real or imaginary helplessness in fulfilling these aspirations. He classified these aspirations and described the ones associated with the oral level as "the need to get affection, to be loved, to be taken care of, to get the 'supplies,' or by the opposite defensive need: to be independent, self-supporting." In his view those associated with the anal level are "the wish to be good, not to be resentful, hostile, defiant, but to be loving, not to be dirty but to be clean, etc." He characterized the aspirations associated with the phallic phase as "the wish to be strong, superior, great, secure, not to be weak and insecure."

Jacobson conceptualized the variables on which self-esteem depends in somewhat different terms. As she saw it, pathology in one or another of the superego, the ego functions, the ego ideal and the self-representations may be reflected in fluctuations of self-esteem and of mood.

4.

Careful observers have long cautioned that in depressions, improvement with psychotherapy should not be confused with validation of specific psychodynamics or theories. Clark (1923), for example, made no secret of his chagrin concerning the results of psychoanalytic treatment of manic-depressives. He states: "It is interesting and at the same time discomforting to the analyst to review what the members of this group indicate afterward what really helped them most as the result of treatment. They all state it was the transference and none are able to give any accurate or precise statement of the main faults disclosed in the analysis."

Kaufman (1937), reporting on the improvement after psychoanalysis in two patients with late-life depressions, emphasized "that probably the most important factor in the improvement of these patients was the transference relationships, and one might put them down as 'transference cures.' "

Jacobson (1954b) makes similar observations about her patients and supplies a more complete theoretical explanation of the situation. She notes that treatment may begin with a marked positive transference in which the patient attributes magical therapeutic qualities to his idealized physician. In this mood of renewed—but unrealistic—optimism, the patient's depression may lift and he may enter a phase of well-being colored by hope and confidence. It is the improvement in this phase that Jacobson categorizes as spurious. No genuine change has occurred in the patient's personality structure and improvement has taken place purely for transference reasons.

These writers were very clear that symptomatic improvements could and did occur primarily as a result of the relationship between the patient and his therapist and that they were curiously unrelated to the resolution of any of the patient's real problems. Symptomatic improvements of this kind are not to be dismissed as unimportant. To the patient they are very important. But they are not necessarily due to any significant modification of the patient's personality structure.

5.

The writer has from time to time indicated that the literature on depression has not grown and flourished independently of the development of general analytic theory. Instead, it represents the application to the depressed states of insights and conceptualizations derived from advances in the general body of analytic theory. Each step forward in psychoanalytic theory has been followed by a renewed consideration of depression with a further gain in understanding.

Abraham started off by seeing depression in the light of Freud's insights into psychosexual development. Freud was able to apply his grasp of the vicissitudes of aggression to the symptomatology of the melancholic. Rado recast analytic thinking on depression in the framework of Freud's new structural concepts. And Gero took advantage of Reich's contribution on the subject of character analysis to discuss depression from this point of view.

Melanie Klein focused attention on the importance of object relationships in depression. Fairbairn and Cohen, disparate as they are in their theoretical allegiances, have nevertheless expanded our understanding of the interpersonal and object relationships of depressed individuals. And Jacobson has worked out most comprehensively of all the implications for depression inherent in the advances in structural theory and ego psychology.

The increasing sophistication of analytic concepts has added to our understanding of the depressive reactions. But it has done more than that. It has focused attention on gaps in our knowledge and in our theory, gaps which were harder to discern when the theoretical framework, although more primitive, was more of a closed system.

6.

After having reviewed this extensive body of literature with its many theoretical disagreements it should be emphasized that an impressive consensus, nevertheless, exists.

There is no basic disagreement for example about how a child acquires the blissful certainty of being loved and wanted with its accompanying sense of security and self-esteem. It is now clear that this desirable outcome is mainly the result of fortunate relationships with the first love objects. Furthermore there is wide agreement that until this happy state of affairs is reached the infant is recurringly overwhelmed by what can best be described in adultomorphic terms as feelings of abandonment, loss, loneliness, depression and anxiety.

The importance of parental and in particular maternal attitudes for the development of emotional security in the child is now taken for granted. It is also becoming clearer that maternal attitudes can be influenced in turn by the behavior of the infant which depends, among other things, on its inherited or acquired activity patterns, disabilities and rudimentary temperament. This results in a relationship which is much more complex than was originally postulated.

It is now clear that severe early deprivation results in very pathological personality development. However no correlation between such early experiences and any particular kind of adult depressive reaction has as yet been established.

Most writers feel that the predisposition to some types of depressive illness includes more than psychological factors. There is, in particular, considerable evidence for a hereditary predisposition to the manic-depressive psychotic reaction; far less evidence exists for hereditary factors in other depressive states.

There is, nevertheless, a consensus that in even the most "endogenous" of depressions, emotional factors play a highly significant role. The onset of the illness can frequently be correlated with situations of loss or disappointment or with circumstances that have these meanings for the patient.

These situations of loss or disappointment producing severe mood disturbances in predisposed individuals as well as less pronounced fluctuations of mood in other people are now generally considered to represent fluctuations in self-esteem.

However, it has become clear in recent years that a psychotic depression consists of more than simply a fall in self-esteem and represents more than a regression to an infantile mode of behavior. Somatic manifestations are often found as well as alterations in reality testing and ego identifications. To describe these changes as regressive is to emphasize their resemblance to infantile states. But to describe them so simply is to overlook the profound difference that exists between a psychotic condition and the modes of functioning of infants and children.

Finally there is a consensus that the term "depression" is applied to a variety of affective states. These states differ not only objectively but subjectively as well. People are depressed in different ways. They experience and manifest and describe their depressions differently. The subjective affective state of the guilty, self-reproachful agitated involutional patient is clearly different from that of the hopeless, futile, retarded schizoid adolescent, although both of these refer to themselves as depressed.

7.

This book represents the summary of an era. This era was chiefly characterized by boldly speculative theoretical formulations and by insightful clinical studies. It was a richly productive era in which sensitive and intuitive observers mapped out whole continents of the mind that had previously been unexplored. It was an era of large scale conceptualizations and generalizations.

This era is drawing to a close. The theories and the categories which were so characteristic of it are now being subjected to critical reappraisal. There are increasing demands for responsible sober testing of theories and hypotheses. Brown (1958) for example in his reflections on psychosomatic medicine has referred to the tendency to deal "with what is essentially a body of shrewdly conceived hypotheses as if they were established principles and laws of human behavior rather than hypotheses per se which need more careful experimental validation."

Stunkard (1959) too has pointed to "a growing tendency to question the usefulness of the high-level abstractions which have so preoccupied psychiatric thinking in the past." He feels that "the emphasis is shifting away from efforts to elucidate final causes, and toward the investigation of intermediary mechanisms. In terms of logical method this shift is away from reliance upon deductions from first principles and in the direction of inductions from clearly defined events."

This shift is to be seen also in the study of depression. The careful investigation into manic-depressive illness carried out by Mabel

Blake Cohen and her colleagues may well be but the first of a series of studies designed to examine the psychodynamic factors in the various depressive reactions. Other experienced investigators (e.g., Beck and Hurvich, 1959), are only now begining to put psychoanalytic hypotheses about depression to the test in empirical studies. And the details of the intrafamilial patterns of depressed patients have yet to be worked out as for example Lidz (1958) is doing in his investigation into family patterns in schizophrenia.

Enough plausible hypotheses about depression have been produced to enable good clinical studies to be carried out. One may confidently predict that the coming years will see an increasing number of such investigations.

However it looks as if the depressive reactions will be studied from several additional points of view. It is beginning to appear as if the subject is much more complex than the early closed system theories would have led one to suspect. The frequently striking success of electro-convulsive therapy in the psychotic depressive reactions was disappointingly unproductive of leads into the physiology of depression. But as this book is going to press anti-depressive drugs are appearing on the scene in greater numbers and with increasing effectiveness. It seems inevitable that any success that these drugs may have will give impetus to the investigation of depression from a wide variety of points of view: the pharmacological, biochemical, neuro-physiological and experimental psychological investigation of depression. If the vast increase in research following the entry of the tranquilizers into psychiatry is any guide, we can expect a flood of new work on depression.

BIBLIOGRAPHY

1. ABRAHAM, KARL: Notes on the Psychoanalytic Investigation and Treatment of Manic-Depressive Insanity and Allied Conditions. In *Selected Papers on Psychoanalysis*. London, The Hogarth Press and the Institute of Psychoanalysis, 1911.

2. ABRAHAM, KARL: The First Pregenital Stage of the Libido. In *Selected Papers on Psychoanalysis*. London, The Hogarth Press and the Institute of Psychoanalysis, 1916.

3. ABRAHAM, KARL: A Short Study of the Development of the Libido. In *Selected Papers on Psychoanalysis*. London, The Hogarth Press and the Institute of Psychoanalysis, 1924.

4. ALEXANDER, FRANZ: *Psychosomatic Medicine; its Principles and Applications*. New York, Norton, 1950.

5. ASCHER, EDOUARD: A criticism of the concept of neurotic depression. *Am. J. Psychiat., 108*:901-908, 1952.

6. BALINT, MICHAEL: New beginning and the paranoid and the depressive syndromes. *Int. J. Psycho-Analysis, 33*:214-224, 1952.

7. BARKAS, M. P.: Treatment of psychotic patients in institutions in the light of psychoanalysis. *Jour. Neurol. and Psychopath., 5*:333-340, 1925.

8. BECK, AARON, T. and HURVICH, MARVIN, S.: Psychological correlates of depression. *Psychosom. Med., 21*:50-55, 1959.

9. BELLAK, LEOPOLD: *Manic-Depressive Psychosis and Allied Conditions*. New York, Grune and Stratton, 1952.

10. BENDER, L.: Psychopathic Behavior Disorders in Children. In *Handbook of Correctional Psychology* (Eds. R. M. Lindner and R. V. Seliger). New York. 1952.

11. BENEDEK, THERESE: Instincts, Drives and Affects. In *Mid-Century Psychiatry*. (Ed. Roy R. Grinker). Springfield, Thomas, 1953.

12. BENEDEK, THERESE: Toward the biology of the depressive constellation. *J. Am. Psa. Assoc., 4*:389-427, 1956.

13. BERES, DAVID: Vicissitudes of superego functions and superego precursors in childhood. *Psychoanalytic Study of the Child, 13*:324-351, 1950.

14. BIBRING, EDWARD: The Mechanism of Depression. In *Affective Disorders.* (Ed. Phyllis Greenacre). New York, International Universities Press, 1953.

15. BLANCO, I. M.: On introjection and the process of psychic metabolism. *Int. J. Psycho-Analysis, 22*:17-36, 1941.

16. BLEULER, EUGEN: *Dementia Praecox or the Group of Schizophrenias.* English translation: New York, International Universities Press, 1950.

17. BOWLBY, J.: Forty-four juvenile thieves: their characters and home-life. *Int. J. Psycho-Analysis, 25*:19-53, 107-128, 1944.

18. BOWLBY, J.: *Maternal Care and Mental Health.* Geneva, World Health Organization, 1952.

19. BRIERLEY, MARJORIE: "Internal objects" and theory. *Int. J. Psycho-Analysis, 22*:107-112, 1941.

20. BRODY, SYLVIA: *Patterns of Mothering.* New York, International Universities Press, 1956.

21. BROWN, FRED: A clinical psychologist's perspective on research in psychosomatic medicine. *Psychosom. Med., 20*:174-180, 1958.

22. CARVER, ALFRED: Notes on the analysis of a case of melancholia. *J. Neurol. and Psychopathology, 1*:320-324, 1921.

23. CLARK, L. PIERCE: The mechanism of periodic mental depressions as shown in two cases, and the therapeutic advantages of such studies. *Rev. Neurol. and Psychiat., 12*:433-448, 1914.

24. CLARK, L. PIERCE: The psychologic treatment of retarded depressions. *Am. J. Insan., 75*:407-410, 1919.

25. CLARK, L. PIERCE: In a symposium on manic-depressive psychosis. *J. Nerv. and Ment. Dis., 57*:162-165, 1923.

26. COHEN, MABEL BLAKE, BAKER, GRACE, COHEN, ROBERT A., FROMM-REICHMANN, FRIEDA, and WEIGERT, EDITH V.: An intensive study of twelve cases of manic-depressive psychosis. *Psychiatry, 17*:103-138, 1954.

27. DEUTSCH, HELENE: *Psychoanalysis of the Neuroses.* Chapter XI. London, The Hogarth Press and the Institute of Psychoanalysis, 1932.

28. *Diagnostic and Statistical Manual, Mental Disorders.* Washington, American Psychiatric Association, 1952.

29. DREYFUS (1907) Referred to in Hoch and Mac Curdy: *Arch. Neurol. & Psychiat.*, 7:1-37, 1922.

30. ENGEL, GEORGE L.: Studies of ulcerative colitis II. The nature of the somatic processes and the adequacy of psychosomatic hypotheses. *Am. J. Medicine, 16*:416-433, 1954.

31. ENGEL, GEORGE L.: Studies of ulcerative colitis III. The nature of the psychologic processes. *Am. J. Medicine, 19*:231-256, 1955.

32. ENGEL, GEORGE L.: Paper read at Psychosomatic Meeting, Atlantic City, N. J., 1955.

33. ENGEL, GEORGE L. and REICHSMAN, FRANZ: Spontaneous and experimentally induced depression in an infant with a gastric fistula. *J. Am. Psa. Assoc.*, 4:428-452, 1956.

34. ERIKSON, ERIK H.: *Childhood and Society*. New York, Norton, 1950.

35. FAIRBAIRN, W. RONALD D.: *Psychoanalytic Studies of the Personality*. London, Tavistock Publications Limited, 1952.

36. FAIRBAIRN, W. RONALD D.: Observations in defence of the object-relations theory of the personality. *Brit. J. M. Psychol.*, 28:144-156, 1955.

37. FEIGENBAUM, DORIAN: A case of hysterical depression. *Psychoanalyt. Rev.*, 13:404-423, 1926.

38. FENICHEL, OTTO: Ueber respiratorische Introjektion. *Internat. Ztschr. f. Psychoanal.*, 17:234-255, 1931.

39. FENICHEL, OTTO: The scoptophilic instinct and identification. *Int. J. Psycho-Analysis, 18*, 1937, quoted in Lewin: *The Psychoanalysis of Elation*. New York, Norton, 1950.

40. FENICHEL, OTTO: *The Psychoanalytic Theory of Neurosis*. New York, Norton, 1945.

41. FREUD, SIGMUND: Further Remarks on the Defence Neuro-Psychoses. 1896, in *Collected Papers*, Vol. 1. London, The Hogarth Press and the Institute of Psychoanalysis.

42. FREUD, SIGMUND: Notes Upon a Case of Obsessional Neurosis. 1909, In *Collected Papers*, Vol. III. London, Hogarth Press and the Institute of Psychoanalysis.

43. FREUD, SIGMUND: Three Essays on Sexuality. 1910, *The Complete Psychological Works of Sigmund Freud*. London, The Hogarth Press and the Institute of Psychoanalysis, 1955.

44. FREUD, SIGMUND: Psychoanalytic Notes upon an Autobiographical Account of a Case of Paranoia. 1911, In *Collected Papers*,

Vol. III. London, Hogarth Press and the Institute of Psychoanalysis.

45. FREUD, SIGMUND: On Narcissim: An Introduction. 1914, In *Collected Papers*, Vol. IV. London, The Hogarth Press and the Institute of Psychoanalysis.

46. FREUD, SIGMUND: Mourning and Melancholia. 1917, In *Collected Papers*, Vol. IV. London, The Hogarth Press and the Institute of Psychoanalysis.

47. FREUD, SIGMUND: *The Ego and the Id*. London, Institute of Psychoanalysis and the Hogarth Press, 1927.

48. FREUD, SIGMUND: *The Problem of Anxiety*. New York, The Psychoanalytic Quarterly Press and Norton, 1936.

49. FRIES, MARGARET E.: Psychosomatic relations between mother and infant. *Psychosom. Med., 6*:159-162, 1944.

50. FRIES, MARGARET E.: The child's ego development and training of adults in his environment. *Psychoanalytic Study of the Child, 2*:85-112, 1946.

51. FRIES, MARGARET E. and WOLF, PAUL J.: Some hypotheses on the role of the congenital activity type in personality development. *Psychoanalytic Study of the Child, 8*:48-62, 1953.

52. FUCHS, S. H.: On introjection. *Int. J. Psycho-Analysis, 18*:269-293, 1937.

53. GARMA, ANGEL: Psychoanalytic Investigations in Melancholia and Other Types of Depressions. In *The Yearbook of Psychoanalysis*, Vol. 3. New York, International Universities Press, 1947.

54. GELEERD, ELISABETH R.: The psychoanalysis of a psychotic child. *Psychoanalytic Study of the Child, 3/4*:311-332, 1949.

55. GERO, GEORGE: The construction of depression. *Int. J. Psycho-Analysis, 17*:423-461, 1936.

56. GERO, GEORGE: An Equivalent of Depression: Anorexia. In *Affective Disorders*. (Ed. Phyllis Greenacre) New York, International Universities Press, 1953.

57. GILLESPIE, R. D.: The clinical differentiation of types of depression. *Guy's Hosp. Reports, 79*:306, 1930.

58. GITELSON, MAXWELL: Re-evaluation of the role of the oedipus complex. *Int. J. Psycho-Analysis, 33*:351-354, 1952.

59. GLOVER, EDWARD: Examination of the Klein system of child psychology. *Psychoanalytic Study of the Child, 1*:75-118, 1945.

60. GLOVER, EDWARD: *The Technique of Psycho-Analysis.* New York, International Universities Press, 1955.

61. GOLDFARB, WILLIAM: Effects of psychological deprivation in infancy and subsequent stimulation. *Am. J. Psychiat., 102*:18-33, 1945.

62. GOOD, R.: Depression. *Brit. J. M. Psychol., 20*:344-375, 1946.

63. GREENACRE, PHYLLIS: Respiratory incorporation and the phallic phase. *Psychoanalytic Study of the Child, 6*:180-205, 1951.

64. GUNTRIP, H.: A Study of Fairbairn's theory of schizoid reactions. *Brit. J. M. Psychol., 25*:86-103, 1952.

65. HARTMANN, HEINZ, KRIS, ERNST, and LOEWENSTEIN, R. M.: Notes on the theory of aggression. *Psychoanalytic Study of the Child, 3/4*:9-36, 1949.

66. HARTMANN, HEINZ: Comments on the psychoanalytic theory of the ego. *Psychoanalytic Study of the Child, 5*:74-96, 1950.

67. HARTMANN, HEINZ: Notes on the theory of sublimation. *Psychoanalytic Study of the Child, 10*:9-29, 1955.

68. HENDERSON, SIR DAVID and GILLESPIE, R. D.: *A Text-Book of Psychiatry,* Seventh Edition. London, Oxford University Press, 1950.

69. HOCH, AUGUST and KIRBY, GEORGE H.: A clinical study of psychoses characterized by distressed perplexity. *Arch. Neurol. and Psychiat., 1*:415-458, 1919.

70. HOCU, AUGUST: *Benign Stupors.* New York, The MacMillan Co., 1921.

71. HOCH, AUGUST and MAC CURDY, JOHN T.: The prognosis of involutional melancholia. *Arch. Neurol. and Psychiat., 7*:1-37, 1922.

72. HOCH, PAUL and POLATIN, PHILIP: Pseudoneurotic forms of schizophrenia. *Psychiatric Quart., 28*:248-276, 1949.

73. HOCH, PAUL and RACHLIN, H. L.: An evaluation of manic-depressive psychosis in the light of follow-up studies. *Am. J. Psychiat., 97*:831-843, 1941.

74. HOCHE: (1910) Quoted in Lewis: Melancholia. *J. Ment. Sc., 80*, 1934.

75. HORNEY, KAREN: *The Neurotic Personality of Our Time.* New York, Norton, 1936.

76. JACOBSON, EDITH: Depression: the oedipus complex in the development of depressive mechanisms. *Psychoanalyt. Quart., 12*:541-560, 1943.

77. JACOBSON, EDITH: The effect of disappointment on ego and

superego formation in normal and depressive development. *Psychoanalyt. Rev., 33*:129-147, 1946.

78. JACOBSON, EDITH: Contribution to the Metapsychology of Cyclothymic Depression. In *Affective Disorders.* (Ed. Phyllis Greenacre) New York, International Universities Press, 1953.

79. JACOBSON, EDITH: The Affects and Their Pleasure-Unpleasure Qualities in Relation to the Psychic Discharge Processes. In *Drives, Affects, Behavior* (Ed. Rudolph M. Loewenstein) New York, International Universities Press, 1953a.

80. JACOBSON, EDITH: Contribution to the metapsychology of psychotic identifications. *J. Am. Psa. Asso., 2*:239-262, 1954.

81. JACOBSON, EDITH: Transference problems in the psychoanalytic treatment of severely depressive patients. *J. Am. Psa. A., 2*:595-606, 1954a.

82. JACOBSON, EDITH: The self and the object world: vicissitudes of their infantile cathexes and their influences on ideational and affective development. *Psychoanalytic Study of the Child, 9*:75-127, 1954b.

83. JACOBSON, EDITH: On normal and pathological moods. *Psychoanalytic Study of the Child, 12*:73-113, 1957.

84. JONES, R. O.: Depressive reactions: their importance in clinical medicine. *Canad. M. A. J., 60*:44-48, 1949.

85. KALLMAN, FRANZ J.: Genetics in relation to mental disorders. *J. Ment. Sc., 94*:250-257, 1948.

86 KALLMAN, FRANZ J.: *Heredity in Health and Mental Disorder.* New York, Norton, 1953.

87. KAUFMAN, IRVING: Three basic sources for pre-delinquent character. *Nerv. Child., 11*:12-15, 1955.

88. KAUFMAN, IRVING and MAKKAY, ELIZABETH: Paper read at annual meeting of American Orthopsychiatric Association, 1955.

89. KAUFMAN, IRVING: Relationship between therapy of children and superego development. In Panel report on superego development and pathology in childhood. *J. Am. Psa. Assoc., 6*:540-551, 1958.

90. KAUFMAN, IRVING and HEIMS, LORA: The body image of the juvenile delinquent. *Am. J. Orthopsychiat., 28*:146-159, 1958.

91. KAUFMAN, M. RALPH: Psychoanalysis in late life depressions. *Psychoanalyt. Quart., 6*:308-335, 1937.

92. KENNEDY, F. (1944) The neuroses: related to the manic-depressive constitution. *Med. Clin. of N. A., 28*:452-466, 1944.

93. KIRBY, G. H.: *State Hosp. Bull., 1*:459, 1908-1909. Quoted in Titley: *Arch. Neurol. & Psychiat., 36*:19-33, 1936.

94. KLEIN, MELANIE: *The Psychoanalysis of Children*. London, The Hogarth Press and the Institute of Psychoanalysis, 1932.

95. KLEIN, MELANIE: A contribution to the Psychogenesis of Manic-Depressive States. 1934, In Melanie Klein, 1948.

96. KLEIN, MELANIE: Mourning and Its Relation to Manic-Depressive States. 1940, In Melanie Klein, 1948.

97. KLEIN, MELANIE: *Contributions to Psycho-Analysis 1921-1945*. London, The Hogarth Press and the Institute of Psychoanalysis, 1948.

98. KNIGHT, ROBERT P.: Introjection, projection and identification. *Psychoanalyt. Quart., 9*:334-341, 1940.

99. KNIGHT, ROBERT P.: Borderline States. *Bull. Menninger Clin., 17*:1-12, 1953.

100. KRAEPELIN, EMIL: (1894) Quoted in Meyer: A Review of Recent Problems in Psychiatry. 1904.

101. KRAEPELIN, EMIL: *Clinical Psychiatry*. New York, Mac Millan Co., 1902.

102. KRAEPELIN, EMIL: (1920) Quoted in Lewis: *J. Ment. Sc., 80*:277-378, 1934.

103. KRETSCHMER, E.: *Physique and Character*. New York, Harcourt, Brace, 1931.

104. KUBIE, L. S.: The fallacious use of quantitative concepts in dynamic psychology. *Psychoanalyt. Quart., 16*:507-518, 1947.

105. KUBIE, LAWRENCE S.: Problems and Techniques of Psychoanalytic Validation and Progress. In *Psychoanalysis as Science* (Ed. E. Pumpian-Mindlin). Stanford University Press, Stanford, 1952.

106. LAMPL-DE GROOT, JEANNE: Depression and Aggression. In *Drives, Affects, Behavior* (Ed. Rudolph M. Loewenstein) New York, International Universities Press, 1953.

107. LEWIN, BERTRAM D.: Kotschmieren, Menses und Weibliches Ueberich. *Int. Ztschr. f. Psa., 16,* 1930, Quoted in Lewin: *The Psychoanalysis of Elation*. New York, Norton, 1950.

108. LEWIN, BERTRAM D.: *The Psychoanalysis of Elation*. New York, Norton, 1950.

109. LEWIS, AUBREY: Melancholia: a historical review. *J. Ment. Sc., 80*:1-42, 1934a.

110. LEWIS, AUBREY: Melancholia: a clinical survey of depressive states. *J. Ment. Sc., 80*:277-378, 1934b.

111. LEWIS, NOLAN D. C. and HUBBARD, LOIS D.: The mechanisms and prognostic aspects of the manic-depressive-schizophrenic combinations. *Assn. for Research in Nervous and Mental Diseases, 11*:471-538, 1931.

112. LEWIS, NOLAN D. C. and PIOTROWSKI, ZYGMUNT: Clinical Diagnosis of Manic-Depressive Psychosis. In *Depression* (Eds. Paul H. Hoch and Joseph Zubin). New York, Grune and Stratton, 1954.

113. LIDZ, THEODORE: Schizophrenia and the family. *Psychiatry, 21*:21-27, 1958.

114. LORAND, SANDOR: *Technique of Psychoanalytic Therapy.* New York, International Universities Press, Inc., 1946.

115. LORENZ, KONRAD: in Discussion, in *Group Processes, Transactions of the First Conference.* New York, Josiah Macy, Jr. Foundation, 1955, Page 18.

116. LOWREY, LAWSON: Personality distortion and early institutional care. *Am. J. Orthopsychiat., 10*:576-585, 1940.

117. MAC CURDY, JOHN T.: in Editor's Preface to Hoch: *Benign Stupors.* New York, The Macmillan Co., 1921.

118. MAHLER, MARGARET: On child psychosis and schizophrenia. *Psychoanalytic Study of the Child, 8*:286-306, 1952.

119. MALAMUD, M., SANDS, G. L., and MALAMUD, I.: The involutional psychoses: a socio-psychiatric study. *Psychosom. Med., 3*:410-426, 1941.

120. MAPOTHER, E.: Manic-depressive psychosis. *Brit. M. J., 2*:872-879, 1926.

121. MAUDSLEY, HENRY: (1895) *The Pathology of Mind,* Third Edition. Referred to in Lewis: Melancholia. *J. Ment. Sci.,* 1934a.

122. MAYER-GROSS, W., SLATER, ELIOT, and ROTH, MARTIN: *Clinical Psychiatry.* London, Cassel and Co., 1954.

123. MCCLARY, ALLAN R., MEYER, EUGENE, and WEITZMAN, ELLIOT, L.: Observations on the role of the mechanism of depression in some patients with disseminated lupus erythematosus. *Psychosom. Med., 17*:311-321, 1955.

124. MEYER, ADOLF: A Review of the Signs of Degeneration and of Methods of Registration. 1895, In *The Collected Papers of Adolf Meyer,* Vol. 2. Baltimore, The Johns Hopkins Press, 1951.

125. MEYER, ADOLF: A Few Trends in Modern Psychiatry. 1904a,

In *The Collected Papers of Adolf Meyer,* Vol. 2. Baltimore, The Johns Hopkins Press, 1951.

126. MEYER, ADOLF: A Review of Recent Problems of Psychiatry. 1904b, In *The Collected Papers of Adolf Meyer,* Vol. 2. Baltimore, The Johns Hopkins Press, 1951.

127. MEYER, ADOLF: The Problems of Mental Reaction Types. 1908, In *The Collected Papers of Adolf Meyer,* Vol. 2. Baltimore, The Johns Hopkins Press. 1951.

128. MEYER, ADOLF: Pathology of Mental Diseases. 1916, In *The Collected Papers of Adolf Meyer,* Vol. 2. Baltimore, The Johns Hopkins Press, 1951.

129. MEYER, ADOLF: Constructive Formulation of Schizophrenia. 1921, In *The Collected Papers of Adolf Meyer,* Vol. 2. Baltimore, The Johns Hopkins Press, 1951.

130. NACHT, S.: in Symposium on mutual influences in development of ego and id. *Psychoanalytical Study of the Child,* 7:54-59, 1952.

131. NISSL, F.: Quoted in Meyer, Adolf: A Few Trends in Modern Psychiatry, 1904.

132. NOYES, ARTHUR P.: *Modern Clinical Psychiatry,* Third Edition. Philadelphia, W. B. Saunders Company, 1948.

133. PALMER, HAROLD D. and SHERMAN, STEPHEN H.: The involutional melancholia process. *Arch. Neurol. and Psychiat.,* 40:762-788, 1938.

134. PECK, MARTIN W.: Notes on identification in a case of depression: reaction to the death of a love object. *Psychoanalyt. Quart.,* 8:1-17, 1939.

135. PENROSE, L. S.: *Digest Neurol. Psychiat.,* 13:644, 1945, Quoted in *Recent Progress in Psychiatry* (Ed. G. W. T. H. Fleming). London, J. & A. Churchill, Ltd., 1950.

136. RACHLIN, H. L.: A follow-up of Hoch's benign stupor cases. *Am. J. Psychiat.,* 92:531-558, 1935.

137. RACHLIN, H. L.: A statistical study of benign stupor in five New York state hospitals. *Psychiat. Quart.,* 11:436-444, 1937.

138. RADO, SANDOR: The problem of melancholia. *Int. J. Psycho-Analysis,* 9:420-438, 1928.

139. RADO, SANDOR: Psychodynamics of depression from the etiologic point of view. *Psychosom. Med.,* 13:51-55, 1951.

140. RANK, BEATA: Aggression. *Psychoanalytic Study of the Child,* 3/4:43-48, 1949.

141. RAPAPORT, DAVID: On the psychoanalytic theory of affects. *Int. J. Psycho-Analysis, 34*:1-22, 1953.

142. REICH, ANNIE: Narcissistic object choice in women. *J. Am. Psa. Assoc., 1*:22-44, 1953.

143. REICH, ANNIE: Early identifications as archaic elements in the superego. *J. Am. Psa. Assoc., 2*:218-238, 1954.

144. REICH, WILHELM: *Character-Analysis; Principles and Techniques for Psychoanalysts in Practise and in Training.* Translated by Theodore P. Wolfe, 2nd. ed. New York, Orgone Institute Press, 1945.

145. RENNIE, T. A. C.: Prognosis in manic-depressive psychosis. *Am. J. Psychiat., 98*:801-814, 1942.

146. REYNELL, W. R.: *Proc. Roy. Soc. Med., 23*:889-890, 1930.

147. RICKMAN, JOHN: Methodology and research in psychopathology. *Br. J. M. Psychol., 24*:1-7, 1951.

148. RIVIERE, JOAN: A contribution to the analysis of negative therapeutic reaction. *Int. J. Psycho-Analysis, 17*:304-320, 1936.

149. ROCHLIN, GREGORY: The disorder of depression and elation. *J. Am. Psa. Assoc., 1*:438-457, 1953.

150. ROCHLIN, GREGORY: Loss and restitution. *Psychoanalytic Study of the Child, 8*:288-309, 1953.

151. ROGERSON, D. H.: (1940) The differentiation of neuroses and psychoses with special reference to states of depression and anxiety. *J. Ment. Sc., 86*:632-644, 1940.

152. SHAGASS, CHARLES, NAIMAN, JAMES, and MILALIK, JOSEPH: An objective test which differentiates between neurotic and psychotic depression. *Arch. Neurol. & Psychiat., 75*:461-471, 1956.

153. SILVERBERG, WILLIAM V.: *Childhood Experience and Personal Destiny.* New York, Springer Publishing Co., 1952.

154. SPERRY, WARREN M.: The Biochemistry of Depressions. In *Depression* (Eds. Paul H. Hoch and Joseph Zubin). New York, Grune and Stratton, 1954.

155. SPITZ, RENÉ A.: Anaclitic depression. *Psychoanalytic Study of the Child, 2*:313-341, 1946.

156. SPITZ, RENÉ A.: Aggression: Its Role in the Establishment of Object Relations, In *Drives, Affects, Behavior* (Ed. Rudolph M. Loewenstein) New York, International Universities Press, 1953.

157. STENGEL, E.: A study on some clinical aspects of the relation-

ship between obsessional neurosis and psychotic reaction types. *J. Ment. Sc., 91*:166-187, 1945.

158. STENGEL, E.: Some clinical observations on psychodynamic relationship between depression and obsessive-compulsive symptoms. *J. Ment. Sc., 94*:166-187, 1948.

159. STRAUSS, E. B.: *Proc. Roy. Soc. Med., 23*:894-895, 1930.

160. STRONGIN, E. L. and HINSIE, L. E.: A method for differentiating manic-depressive depressions from other depressions by means of parotid secretions. *Psychiat. Quart., 13*:697-704, 1939.

161. STUNKARD, ALBERT J.: The "dieting depression". *Am. J. Med., 23*:77-86, 1957.

162. STUNKARD, ALBERT J.: Research in obesity. *Bull. of the Johns Hopkins Hosp.* (in press), 1959.

163. SULLIVAN, HARRY STACK: *Conceptions of Modern Psychiatry.* Washington, The William Alanson White Psychiatric Foundation, 1947.

164. SULLIVAN, HARRY STACK: *The Interpersonal Theory of Psychiatry.* New York, Norton, 1953.

165. TITLEY, W. B.: Prepsychotic personality of patients with involutional melancholia. *Arch. Neurol. and Psychiat., 36*:19-33, 1936.

166. TREDGOLD, R. F.: Depressive states in the soldier. *Brit. M. J., 2*:109-112, 1941.

167. VAN OPHUIJSEN, J. H. W., On the origin of the feeling of persecution. *Int. J. Psychoanalysis, 1,* 1920, quoted in Lewin: *The Psychoanalysis of Elation,* New York, Norton, 1950.

168. WERNER, HEINZ: *Comparative Psychology of Mental Development.* New York, Folett, 1940.

169. WHITEHORN, JOHN C.: Physiological changes in emotional states. *Assn. for Research in Nervous and Mental Diseases, 19*:256-270, 1930.

170. WHITEHORN, JOHN C.: Psychodynamic Approach to the Study of Psychoses. Chapter IX. In *Dynamic Psychiatry* (Eds. Franz Alexander and Helen Ross). Chicago, Univ. of Chicago Press, 1952.

171. WHITEHORN, JOHN C.: Chairman of Editorial Board, 1952 Conference on Psychiatry Education, *The Psychiatrist, His Training and Development.* Washington, American Psychiatric Association, 1953.

172. WHITEHORN, JOHN C.: *Psychiatric Education and Progress.* Salmon Lecture, 1955, Unpublished.

173. ZETZEL, ELIZABETH R.: The Depressive Position. In *Affective Disorders* (Ed. Phyllis Greenacre) New York, International Universities Press, Inc., 1953.

174. ZILBOORG, GREGORY: Manic-Depressive Psychoses. In *Psycho-Analysis Today* (Ed. Sandor Lorand), New York, Covici-Friede, 1933.

175. ZILBOORG, GREGORY: Ambulatory schizophrenia. *Psychiatry,* 4:149-155, 1941.

176. ZILBOORG, GREGORY: *History of Medical Psychology,* New York, Norton, 1941a.

INDEX

method of ego introjection of objects, 26

Introjection
age at which process occurs, 41
as used by Jacobson, 107
conception of by Jacobson, 107-108
corroboration of by Abraham, 29
defined by Fenichel, 107
defined by Freud, 25
defined by Knight, 107
difference from incorporation, 26
how ego introjects objects, 26
oral method of, 26
role of determining form taken by ego, 41
role in formation of superego, 41

Involutional melancholia
as an independent diagnostic entity, 13
characteristics of prepsychotic, 13, 14
comparison of characteristics of with manic-depressive psychosis, 13-14
difference from prepsychotic personality of manic-depressive, 111
ignorance of from psychoanalytic point of view, 111
principal genetic relationship leading to, 111
question of being a distinct diagnostic category, 110-111
relationship of manic-depressive insanity to, 7
rigid character of person with, 111
theory of Hoch and MacCurdy, 11
benign psychoses of manic-depressive variety, 11
malignant psychoses clinically related to dementia praecox, 11

J

Jacobson, Edith, 52, 56, 57, 58, 61, 63, 64, 65, 66, 67, 68, 69, 70, 71, 72, 73, 76, 78, 79, 81, 82, 83, 84, 85, 94, 97, 99, 104, 106, 107, 108, 110, 111, 112, 114, 115, 129, 132, 133, 134, 135, 138, 140, 141, 142, 143, 151, 152
conception of introjection by, 107-108
conception of mechanism of depression, 140
conception of self-esteem in depression, 141, 142
contribution to study of depression, 56-72
review of, 71-72

introjection as used by, 107
mechanism of melancholia as seen by, 106
results of treatment of depression, 142
studies of schizophrenia by, 114-116
summary of concept of depression, 67-68
contribution to understanding of depression, 143
theory of free intervals of manic-depressives, 94
theory of predisposition to depression, 83
use of term aggression, 99-100
views on handling demandingness of manic-depressive patients, 132-133

Jones, R. O., 120, 152

Juvenile delinquency
as child's method of coping with depression, 120
as defense against depression, 120

K

Kahlbaum, K. L., 9

Kallman, Franz J., 80, 111, 117, 152
theory of heredity factor of manic-depression, 80

Kaufman, Irving, 120, 152

Kaufman, M. Ralph, 111, 142, 152
results of treatment of depression, 142

Kennedy, Foster, 120, 152

Kirby, George H., 10, 11, 151, 153

Klein, Melanie, 40, 41, 42, 43, 44, 45, 46, 47, 72, 73, 74, 76, 79, 83, 84, 85, 87, 88, 89, 91, 95, 96, 107, 113, 114, 129, 132, 139, 143, 153
as founder of English school of psychoanalysis, 40
contribution of to study of depression, 40-47
death instinct as seen by, 95-96
depressive position as seen by, 95
observations of children in oedipal period, 85-86
observations of infants' sadism, 42
theory of aggression in depression, 95-96
theory of depressive position, 113
theory of predisposition to depression, 83
view of depression, 139-140

Knight, Robert P., 13, 107, 115, 153
definition of introjection by, 107